P·LAY

Dance & drama

LARRAINE S. HARRISON

Published by Scholastic Ltd,
Villiers House,
Clarendon Avenue,
Leamington Spa,
Warwickshire CV32 5PR
Text © Larraine S Harrison
© 1998 Scholastic Ltd
2 3 4 5 6 7 8 9 0   9 0 1 2 3 4 5 6 7

Author
Larraine S Harrison

Editor
Jane Bishop

Series designer
Lynne Joesbury

Designer
Claire Belcher

Illustrations
Jenny Tulip

Cover photograph
© Digital Vision

Designed using Adobe Pagemaker

British Library Cataloguing-in-Publication Data
A catalogue record for this book is available from the British Library.

ISBN 0-590-53791-1

CONTENTS

INTRODUCTION

CHAPTER ONE: LANGUAGE AND LITERACY

CHAPTER TWO: MATHEMATICS

CHAPTER THREE: PERSONAL AND SOCIAL DEVELOPMENT

CHAPTER FOUR: KNOWLEDGE AND UNDERSTANDING OF THE WORLD

CHAPTER FIVE: PHYSICAL DEVELOPMENT

CHAPTER SIX: CREATIVE DEVELOPMENT

PHOTOCOPIABLES

Dance

Young children are constantly on the move. They seem to have an innate desire to extend their own physical capabilities, and success in this area is very important to them. Movement is a means of expression which precedes the ability to communicate through speech. Provide every opportunity for children to explore and develop their movement skills within a range of contexts, both structured and unstructured. The structured activities in this book are not intended to replace other opportunities for the children to dance spontaneously to music, songs and rhymes, or in response to a play situation. Children need the freedom to dance in play whenever they want to and this will help to develop their confidence and imagination, while teaching them that physical activity can be enjoyable.

Drama

Children seem to have a built-in urge to role play. This is nature's way of helping them to make sense of the world in which they live. Make sure young children have a range of opportunities to explore role play, unhindered by adult intervention, as well as opportunities to take part in more structured activities. The structured drama activities in this book are designed to complement ongoing opportunities for free play in role play areas, rather than replace them. Choose costumes and props for role play areas with care and change them frequently to stimulate a range of role play situations.

The School Curriculum and Assessment Authority (SCAA) recognises the contribution role play can make to the successful development of language and literacy in its *Desirable Outcomes for Children's Learning*. One of the recommended Desirable Outcomes is that children should make up their own stories and take part in role play with confidence. A rich environment for role play will certainly stimulate the development of language and literacy as well as providing a good basis for more structured drama activities.

Setting up the environment

Children need an environment in which they can practise their emerging physical skills in dance and engage in dramatic activities. Some nursery units are able to use a nearby school hall for dance and drama activities, but other groups are less fortunate and have to make space where they can. Bigger isn't always better though, as large school halls can be very intimidating to young children.

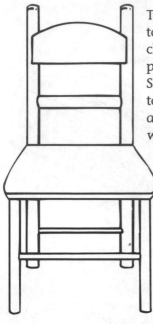

Try and arrange a number of short introductory visits by the children to the hall to sing familiar action songs and rhymes to help the children feel more secure. You could also consider sectioning off part of the hall with benches or chairs, in order to reduce the space. Shiny, smooth floors are attractive to children and the temptation to slide around a very large floor space can be detrimental to the activity. Where a hall is not available, it may be necessary to work with smaller groups in a cleared area of the existing room or in an adjoining room. Outside areas can be problematic if they are too vast or if the children are likely to be distracted by outside noise or activity. These areas are also affected by the weather and cannot provide a permanent solution to finding a space for dance and drama.

Not all drama activities need a large space, but dance activities by their very nature, require the children to move around freely. Whether it be dance or drama, in a hall or in the corner of a room, provide the best available environment for the children to develop their skills.

Storage

Store simple costumes and a few props relevant to a particular theme along with supporting books, tapes and other materials in a labelled box or bag or on hangers. Include notes on how the drama or dance activity is carried out and how it can be followed up. Such storage methods will prove to be a valuable time-saving resource for the following year.

Health and safety

The space – Always make sure that the children understand the boundaries of the space you are to work in. Be specific about anything in the room that will not be part of the activity, such as wall bars in a hall or a computer in a corner. Children often want to use nearby objects as props and are usually unaware of their potential for danger. Be specific, and if necessary, explain why these things are not to be touched. If any children ignore your instructions, stop the activity and tell them again.

Where the activity involves movement, make sure that hard floors are swept and cleaned, especially if the children have bare feet. Movement areas should be free of clutter and away from anything with sharp or jagged edges. Carpeted areas are soft and comfortable for some drama activities but are less suited to dance activities, where friction can cause burns to bare feet or other parts of the body. Hard outside surfaces with no 'give' may also be unsuitable for activities involving heavy movements such as stamping.

Clothing – Encourage children to change or adapt their clothing for dance. They need to wear light comfortable clothing that will not restrict their mobility. This may involve taking things off, rather than a full change of clothing. Bare feet or soft shoes are advisable, but don't let children just wear socks as this can be dangerous and children could slip or trip over. Drama activities do not usually require a change of clothing, but bare feet or indoor shoes are advisable if the activity involves moving around.

Costumes and props – When choosing or making costumes for drama or role play, avoid things tied with strings or laces, as these can become fastened round the neck or pulled too tight. Use Velcro for fastenings where possible. Make sure costumes are regularly washed if worn next to the skin or near the face. Hats can be a problem and should be chosen with washing in mind. Check props for sharp edges.

Using adult helpers

Adult helpers can be a valuable resource, especially where they are asked to support less confident children during a dance or drama activity. Make sure they are careful to avoid directing the children and that they are fully aware of the aims of the activity and the methods involved.

Always recognise and value the contribution which a child's parents or carers can make to the group. Make a list of anyone who is willing to help in any way – by volunteering as a helper, repairing toys or supplying resources such as wool or cardboard and do call upon that help as soon as the need arises. Encourage carers to try activities they may

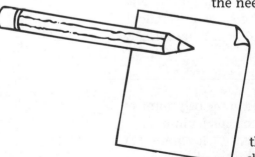

not at first consider, for example clay or woodwork. If they feel uncertain of their abilities in a particular area, offer them the chance to come in and observe regular helpers at work or consider the possibility of offering them a little on-the-job training to boost their confidence.

Even if carers are unable to take an active role in the group on a regular basis it is important that they should not feel isolated or left out. One way to do this is to encourage children to use symbols, pictures or letters to make notes to take home to remind carers of particular events, or items you may be collecting. Use copious signs, posters and fly-sheets to keep everyone up-to date and fully informed about the group's activities. Finally, try to make time to discuss any real concerns or issue genuine praise at the end of every session or send a written message home with the child if you feel the carer is likely to dash away before you have a chance to talk.

The role of the adult

Adults who lead activities will be at times directors, and at other times facilitators, to enable children to make their own explorations. Whatever the activity, it is important that you are both enthusiastic and yet serious about the work. This is particularly important in drama, which relies on the children behaving as if they really were inside the imaginary situation. When taking on the role of a character, always use a small item of clothing, as a clear sign that you are pretending to be someone else. Explain what you are going to do, before taking on the role, to help the children feel more secure. You won't need to talk in a different voice or act in an extreme manner when playing a part, as such behaviour can frighten or amuse the children. All that's needed is a sincere presentation of the character's attitude and feelings. When you want to come out of role, tell the children what you are going to do and take off the item of clothing.

Observation and assessment

Through the dance activities you will be able to assess whether children are physically confident and able to express themselves in movement. You will discover whether they can move in different directions and in different ways and you will be able to assess their spatial awareness. Dance activities also offer opportunities to assess children's listening skills. During drama activities, look for children who can respond appropriately within an imaginary situation and those who are verbally confident.

Links with home

Some of the activities can be adapted into short performances for parents to watch. Such enjoyable events help to encourage links with home and provide opportunities to meet parents on an informal basis.

How to use this book

The chapters in this book are organised into the six Areas of Learning identified for under-fives by the School Curriculum and Assessment Authority (SCAA). Each chapter contains activities for both dance and drama designed for the 'average' four-year-old. Each individual activity includes a statement of the learning objective, a suggested group size and details of what you need and how to set things up. There are also sections on questions to ask and adaptations for younger and older children. Finally there are some suggestions for follow-up activities.

Objectives

Although the one main objective mentioned at the beginning of each activity deals with just one area of the curriculum, most activities will also cover several other areas of learning. For example, language development is a constant and continuous process and is therefore implicit in every activity.

Group size

A guide to the number of children who can be involved in the activity with one adult supervisor is given. This can be adapted to suit your circumstances, the number of adult helpers you have and the maturity of the children.

What you need

Everything you need to complete the main activity is listed but again, it can be adapted to suit your circumstances and the availability of materials.

Setting up

Most activities will require an introductory discussion or instruction period. Some of the ideas may also require a certain amount of preparation such as setting out equipment or labelling various items. It is generally a good idea to try out any practical activities yourself, in advance, so that you will be aware of any difficulties or questions that might arise when the children embark upon the tasks themselves.

What to do

The activity is explained from beginning to end, with explicit instructions as well as general suggestions. Illustrations are provided where further guidance may be necessary.

Questions to ask

This section contains some suggestions for the type of questions you may find useful to ask the children. They are intended to prompt discussion and promote further questions and discussion. Remember to allow time for the children to consider and discuss their own questions as well as those posed by the supervising adult.

For younger children

A suggestion for adapting the activity to suit younger or less able children is offered. You may be able to think of further ideas yourself which are more suited to the particular children in your care.

For older children

An extension of the main activity for use with older or more able children is also provided. Encourage these children to think of their own ways to broaden the scope of the activity if they can. This, in itself, is an excellent exercise in creative thinking.

Follow-up activities

Some suggestions are made for extending or broadening the activity to cover other areas of learning and to spark further ideas of your own or of the children.

Photocopiable activity sheets

One activity from each chapter is accompanied by a photocopiable resource sheet to be found at the back of the book. Some of these are used as part of the main activity while others can be used as a follow-up to that activity. The text offers suggestions for ways in which to use the pages. You may wish to enlarge some of them to A3 size to make it easier for very young children.

Topic web

The following page contains a photocopiable web showing all the activities in the book with the relevant page references.

DANCE AND DRAMA

Dance and drama activities can help children to think about familiar rhymes and stories in more depth, by inviting them to view the events from inside the narrative. Some of the activities can be used to stimulate early mark-making such as writing notes, invitations and posters.

HELPING DADDY BEAR

Learning objective
Drama – to encourage empathy with the Three Bears in the story of Goldilocks.

Group size
Six to 20 children.

What you need
An illustrated version of 'Goldilocks and the Three Bears', writing paper, two pieces of A4 card, a pen and a marker pen.

Setting up
Make a note from Daddy Bear saying:

Make signs saying 'kitchen' and 'bedroom' and place them in two separate areas of your room. Place the note somewhere in the 'kitchen' area. Read the story of 'Goldilocks and the Three Bears' to the children.

What to do
Ask the children to pretend that they are in the Bears' house. Draw their attention to the kitchen and bedroom areas. Pretend to find the note in the kitchen and read it out. Point out the mess caused by spilled porridge in the kitchen. Demonstrate what to do by miming mopping the floor and wiping the table and ask the children to carry out the cleaning as you have done.

After the children have finished, sit them down while you inspect the work. Praise them for their efforts and then move to the 'bedroom'. Point out the mud on the beds caused by Goldilocks' shoes. Ask the children to change the covers on the beds. Now ask them to see if there are any more jobs they can do in the house before they leave. After the drama, send the children a thank you card from the Three Bears.

> Dear children
>
> I am sorry we are not at home but we have gone to town to buy Baby Bear a new chair. Goldilocks has made such a mess in our house that it will take ages to clean up. Please would you be very kind and clean up the mess for us.
>
> Thank you.
> Love from Daddy Bear

Questions to ask
Why does Baby Bear need a new chair? How do you think the Bears felt when they saw the mess? How will the Bears feel when they see all our work?

For younger children
Keep the group small and let the children copy you as you complete each activity.

For older children
After the work has been completed, put on a scarf and play the part of one of Goldilocks' parents. Explain that Goldilocks has come home and will not say what she has been doing. Ask the children if they can tell you what happened. Come out of role by taking off the scarf.

Follow-up activities
● Ask the children to draw pictures of the jobs they did for the Bears. Write a sentence underneath each picture to describe what is happening.
● Wear a jacket and play the role of Daddy Bear. Tell the story of what happened from his point of view.
● Talk about helping at home and keeping things clean.

OPENING DAY

Learning objective
Drama – to write within the context of the role play area.

Group size
Ten to 30 children.

What you need
Items for a role play area providing a public service (hairdressers, railway station, garage, opticians, post office, library, travel agent, café or shop). Sheet of A3 paper, writing and colouring materials or printing facilities.

Setting up
Produce a large drawing of what the role play area will look like, when it is set up. Have some of the materials for the role play area on display.

What to do
Tell the children about the new role play area and show them the drawing and the items which are going to be used. Tell the children that the area will be opening soon and that there will be a special opening day for visitors to look round. Explain that invitations must be sent out and posters put up to let people know about it. Discuss what the invitations should say and what could be on the posters.

Ask the children to work in small groups to make the invitations and posters over the next few days. Try to let the children write their own words as much as possible and let them use pictures to illustrate the facilities on offer. Give the invitations to parents and staff and put up posters. Meanwhile, establish the role play area, involving the children as much as possible.

On opening day, hold a short ceremony with ribbon and scissors and then let the children take turns to play freely in the area in small groups. Organise the visitors to ensure that all groups receive at least one visitor.

Questions to ask
Ask the children to tell you what all the items for the role play area are called and what they are used for. When visiting the role play area, ask questions such as: What does this do? What is this for? and How do you work this?

For younger children
Let the children try out the role play area for free play, in small groups, before opening day.

For older children
Working in small groups, ask the children to take turns to tell everyone what happened to them on opening day. Ask the children to draw and write about this after the discussion.

Follow-up activities
● Observe the children in the role play area and report back to all the children, for example 'I was in the cafe today and this is what I saw…'. Ask the children for their observations too.
● Send imaginary letters from the public relating to the role play area and its services, such as a thank you letter, or a letter of complaint about an aspect of the service that can be rectified.
● Ask the children to draw portraits or pictures of the visitors who came to the opening day. Display these under the heading 'Our Visitors'.

NEW SHOES

Learning objective
*Drama – to develop
speaking skills in a
shoe shop role play.*

Group size
Eight to ten children.

What you need
A selection of different kinds of shoes, an adult's jacket, sufficient chairs for half the group.

Setting up
Show the children the different shoes and start a discussion about buying shoes and different kinds of shoes and shoe sizes. Line up the chairs, as if in a shoe shop.

What to do
Ask the children to pretend that the area in front of them is a shoe shop. Divide the children into two groups so that they can take turns at being shopkeepers and customers.

Discuss how assistants greet the customers as they enter the shop and talk about what tasks they will perform. Explain that you will play the part of the shop owner when you put on the jacket. Support the proceedings where necessary, encouraging all the children to take part. Take off the jacket to stop the drama and let the children change roles.

Questions to ask
Ask each customer what they will ask for when they go to the shoe shop.

When the customers are pretending to try on the shoes, ask questions such as: Do they feel comfortable? Are they too big or too small? Are they too loose or too tight?

For younger children
Direct the drama more closely and work with fewer children.

For older children
Ask the children to draw a picture of the kind of shoes they would like to buy and let them paste their pictures onto the end of an empty shoe box; mark the size on the box too. Use these as props in the drama.

Follow-up activities
● Complete photocopiable page 59, to match the pairs of footwear.
● Bring in an assortment of different kinds of shoes and boots for the children to sort into pairs and by other criteria such as laces, buckles or Velcro fastenings.
● Make a block graph of shoe sizes to find the most common size.
● Link the drama to the story of 'The Elves and the Shoemaker', Brothers Grimm (Ladybird).

ALL THE KING'S MEN

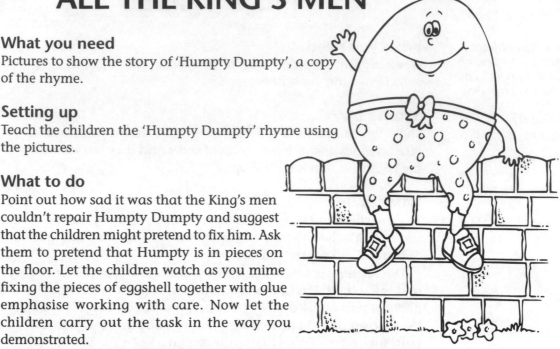

Learning objective
Drama – to explore the rhyme Humpty Dumpty.

Group size
Six to 20 children.

What you need
Pictures to show the story of 'Humpty Dumpty', a copy of the rhyme.

Setting up
Teach the children the 'Humpty Dumpty' rhyme using the pictures.

What to do
Point out how sad it was that the King's men couldn't repair Humpty Dumpty and suggest that the children might pretend to fix him. Ask them to pretend that Humpty is in pieces on the floor. Let the children watch as you mime fixing the pieces of eggshell together with glue emphasise working with care. Now let the children carry out the task in the way you demonstrated.

After a while, announce that Humpty is now in one piece. Explain that Humpty will want to sit on the wall again, but it is too high. Ask the children to knock down some bricks using imaginary hammers from an imaginary shed. When the wall has been lowered, stand round Humpty and on a given signal, lift him onto the wall. Explain that the land below the wall is very hard and if Humpty were to fall again, he would break. Ask the children to suggest what would make his landing softer if he were to fall, and ask them to carry out the necessary work. Direct them to the shed for materials and thank the children when it is complete.

Questions to ask
Ask the children why they think Humpty fell off the wall and why they think the King's men failed to fix him. What kinds of soft materials would break our landings if we fell? (Foam, grass, mats or water.) Discuss the practicality of each suggestion.

For younger children
Work with a small group and keep the discussions short. Let the children copy your actions.

For older children
Suggest that the children travel to the wall on horseback like the King's men. Using mime, demonstrate how to mount a horse carefully and lead the line of horses in a trot around the room, until you announce that you have arrived at the wall where you can set about helping Humpty Dumpty. After completing the tasks, return on the horses and put them in the King's stables to rest.

Follow-up activities
● Talk about the dangers of climbing and sitting on high walls.
● Read *Little Lumpty* by Miko Imai (Walker Books).
● Draw some bricks on a piece of white sheeting and throw it over a box or sturdy table to resemble a low wall. Let the children take turns to act out the rhyme using the wall.

SKIP TO A RHYME

Learning objective
Dance – to learn and enjoy traditional rhymes.

Group size
Six to 30 children.

What you need
Knowledge of a few simple traditional rhymes with strong rhythms, a tambour or similar instrument, a room with enough space for the children to move around.

Setting up
Recite some traditional rhymes with the children and let them clap along with the rhythms.

What to do
Let the children practice skipping around the space and then send them off to skip to a space in the room and sit down. Tell them that when you play the tambour once they must skip around the room, moving without touching anyone. When you play the tambour twice they must stop still like statues. Repeat this until most of the children are able to stop reasonably quickly on the two beats of the tambour. Encourage them to lift their knees and arms as they skip.

Tell them to skip round again as you say a happy rhyme, such as 'Pat-a-cake' or 'Girls and boys come out to play'. They should stop on the tambour as before. Tell them to skip to the rhymes again, making their skipping light and happy. Skip with the children to demonstrate as you recite the rhyme. Skip with light and happy steps to another rhyme such as 'Hickory dickory dock', but this time encourage the children to clap as they skip.

Now suggest that they skip to the next rhyme with bigger, heavier steps. Choose a slower rhyme such as 'Humpty Dumpty' and say it quite slowly, emphasising the rhythm. Repeat this two or three times or until the children have mastered skipping with bigger steps. Then choose another slow rhyme such as 'Doctor Foster', and let them skip to this with big steps. Finally repeat all the rhymes and skip to them again in the same manner as before. Finish by telling the children to skip towards you and sit down.

Questions to ask
How does this rhyme make you feel? Who can show us how to skip happily?

For younger children
Keep to the light and happy rhymes and work on the children's ability to respond to the tambour.

For older children
Ask the children to clap first high and then low as they skip. Let the children skip in pairs, holding hands with their partners for some of the rhymes.

Follow-up activities
● Introduce some established singing and dancing games, such as 'In and out the dusty bluebells' or 'The hokey cokey', see *Oranges and Lemons* by Ian Beck and Karen King (OUP).
● Listen to rhymes set to music on a cassette tape together and encourage the children to clap along to the rhythms.

JACK AND JILL

Learning objective
Drama – to become
familiar with and
identify with the Jack
and Jill rhyme.

Group size
Up to 30 children.

What you need

A picture of Jack and Jill and the well, a chair, a copy of the rhyme 'Ring-o-ring-o-roses'.

Setting up

Teach the children to say the Jack and Jill rhyme. Show the children the picture and make sure they understand what a well is. Organise the children into pairs.

What to do

Ask the children to pretend to walk up a steep hill to fetch some water from a well. Explain that the room will be the hill. Put a chair at one end of the room and ask them to imagine it's a well. Explain that each pair will need to pretend to take a bucket.

Arrange the children in a crocodile formation and walk in a circle to lead the way up the hill. Say the Jack and Jill rhyme as you walk. When you have walked for a while, ask the children to sit with you near the well. Talk about the view from the top of the hill, and the dangers of running down steep hills and falling down. Play 'Ring-o-ring-o-roses', where everyone falls down safely. After the game, arrange the children in a circle around the well. Mime winding a large bucket down the well and fetching up some water. Encourage the children to hold out their buckets as you quickly pour some water into each one. Ask the children to suggest how to avoid falling over and spilling the water on the way down, like Jack and Jill did. Set off down the hill in a crocodile formation and say the rhyme as you go.

At the bottom of the hill, find an imaginary water barrel and let the children pour their water into it.

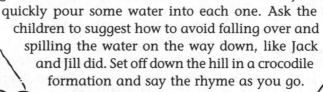

Questions to ask

At the top of the hill ask questions such as Who can see some houses? Who can see some trees? What else can you see? Why do you think Jack and Jill fell over?

For younger children

Do the same activity with a small group and let the children pretend to have a bucket each, but omit talking about the view from the hill.

For older children

Encourage the children to tell you everything that happened to Jack and Jill. Ask them for their advice on how to avoid falling down the hill.

Follow-up activities
● Talk about how Jack tried to mend his head and use it to discuss simple first aid and what to do in an emergency.
● Let small groups of children play with large and small buckets of water to find out the heaviest and lightest when full and empty.

ACTING IT OUT

Learning objective
Drama – to present a story or rhyme to an audience.

Group size
Variable, depending on the story.

What you need
A story or rhyme, a simple piece of costume or an object to represent each character, a few props.

Setting up
Make sure the performers are familiar with the story or rhyme to be performed. Make sure the audience (another group of children and staff) will be able to see everything. Experiment with different arrangements such as putting the actors in the middle of a circle, or arranging the audience in a semicircle or in a V-shape.

What to do
When allocating parts, try to include as many children as possible by using a range of characters including animals, other living things and objects. For example in the rhyme 'Mary, Mary, quite contrary', some children can be silver bells, wearing silver headbands with sleigh bells or finger bells to ring when Mary passes them in her garden. Others can be cockle shells and be given shells to rattle, while the pretty maids can dance or sway as Mary passes. Alternatively, a group of children can play the bells and rattle the shells at the appropriate moments.

Whatever the story or rhyme, try to make the children's contributions simple and make sure that they know exactly when they are to perform their part. If there is a repeated refrain in the story or rhyme, let the audience join in to say the words at the appropriate moments. At the end of every performance, try to give everyone some kind of positive feedback.

Question to ask
Include the children in aspects of the directing, so that they feel involved.

Where do you think this person might stand, behind here or in front of there? How do you think this person might be feeling? Who can show us how to look like this?

For younger children
Limit the performance to simple actions and use very few costumes or props. Keep to a short, well-known rhyme and focus on the children listening for the right cues to move.

For older children
Stop at various points in the narrative to let individual children speak. Encourage them to speak spontaneously in role, but let the group make some prior suggestions as to what kinds of words would be appropriate.

Follow-up activities
● Perform to a wider audience such as a few parents or visitors.
● Ask the children to draw pictures of themselves in role. Write under each picture 'This is ..... He/she is pretending to be ..... in our play'.
● Leave out the costumes and encourage the children to act out the events for themselves in free play without an audience.

LITTLE BOY KRISHNA

Learning objective
Dance – to learn an
Indian style dance.

Group size
Six to 12 children.

What you need
Pictures and items (food, clothes and ornaments) to represent aspects of Indian life and culture, sleigh bells.

Setting up
Use the pictures and artefacts to talk about aspects of Indian life and culture. Use the children's own experiences if appropriate.

What to do
Tell the story (below) in sections and teach the actions as you go. Focus on slow careful movements and appropriate facial expressions. Tell the children that they must start the movements when you ring the bells and stop when the bells stop.

Follow this pattern for each of the sections: say the words/teach the action/practise with the bells/dance to the words and bells.

1. *There was once a little boy called Krishna who lived in a place where there were lots of cows.* Make the hand movement for a cow.

2. *One day Krishna crept secretly into the place where the milk and butter were stored.* Make a few steps and show how Krishna's face might look.

3. *Krishna drank some milk from one of the buckets and dipped his fingers into the butter to taste it.* Make up simple mime actions including facial expressions showing pleasure at the taste.

4. *Krishna heard his mother coming and hid.* Squat down and make a hiding gesture by putting both hands in front of the face, palms facing outwards. Peep from behind the hands and show fear.

5. *Krishna's mother saw the marks in the butter and noticed some spilled milk. She was very cross.* Take up a cross pose, such as hand on hips, and adopt an appropriate facial expression.

6. *Krishna's mother saw Krishna hiding and asked him who had done this to the butter and milk.* Adopt an inquiring stance such as open arms and a puzzled face.

7. *Krishna said that he didn't know, but his mother saw that his face was covered in milk and butter. She was very cross and sent Krishna out.* Adopt the cross pose again, with one outstretched arm, pointing away.

Now go through the whole story and actions again, without stopping.

Questions to ask
How do people look when they are scared/cross/puzzled? How do people stand when they are cross? What do they do with their arms and legs? Let the children show you the answers to these questions by demonstrating with their bodies, as well as using words.

For younger children
Work with a small group. Let the children copy your actions as you tell the story.

For older children
Encourage the children to perform the dance without the words.

Follow-up activities
● Make a storyboard sequence telling the story and let the children draw the pictures.
● Teach the children about milking cows and how butter is made.

MATHEMATICS

Activities in this section use dance and drama to focus on number recognition, sorting, counting and direction. Imaginary contexts and movement are used to create the need for mathematical exploration.

THE NUMBER TWO

Learning objective
Dance – to focus on the number two, using hands and feet movements.

Group size
Up to 30 children.

What you need
A tambour or similar instrument, the words of the song 'If you're happy and you know it'.

Setting up
Prepare the room ready for a movement activity.

What to do
Sing and do the actions for 'If you're happy and you know it clap your hands' together. Encourage the children to try other ways of moving two hands such as shaking, wriggling, rubbing. Ask them to wiggle their fingers. Then ask them if they can wiggle just two fingers and then two thumbs. Now ask the children to let their two hands dance around them as they sit, making them dance very near and far away. As you point to two children, ask them to follow their dancing hands to a space and sit down. Repeat this with other pairs. If there is one child left then make a pair with this child yourself.

Point out that two feet can dance too. When you play the tambour, the children should dance around the room on two feet, being careful not to touch each other. When you stop playing, the children must stop too. Then ask them to think about what else two feet can do. Using the children's suggestions and ideas of your own, continue in this way with other movements, such as walking on two feet with big steps/small steps, tiptoeing, stamping, running, jumping and walking on two heels.

Questions to ask
Two hands can clap. Who can show us another way of moving two hands? Who can wriggle two fingers? Who can wriggle two thumbs?

Two feet can dance. Who can show us another way of moving on two feet? Can you walk on two heels? Can you take big strides on your toes?

For younger children
Play musical bumps using different ways of moving on two feet.

For older children
Make the movements into a sequence involving hands and feet. Give more precise instructions such as 'Skip with light steps' or 'Dance your hands high then low'.

Follow-up activities
● Let the children use paints on their hands and feet to make prints.
● Ask the children to make pictures of their movements and display these with an appropriate text such as 'I am jumping on two feet'.
● Play 'Simon says', making all the movements using two hands and two feet.

POSTING LETTERS

Learning outcome
Drama – to recognise numbers up to ten.

Group size
Five to ten children.

What you need
Thirty used letters that have been resealed, ten pieces of white A4 card, a sheet of A3 paper, a marker pen, a felt-tipped pen, ten chairs.

Setting up
Arrange the chairs in two equal rows, facing each other. Write the numbers one to ten on the cards and place one number on the back of each chair, as they would be numbered on a street. Put up a paper sign saying 'Red Road'. Readdress the letters to Red Road, allocating three letters to each house number.

What to do
Ask the children to pretend that the chairs are the doors of houses on Red Road. Explain that the seats will be the letter boxes. Ask them to pretend that they are new postmen and women learning the job. Pretend to put on uniforms and then go for a walk up and down Red Road to look at the numbers.

Now sit the children on the floor and give out the letters at random, so that each child has at least three. Tell the children to spread their letters out on the floor in front of them and hold up any letters that are for number 1, Red Road. Give these letters to one of the children to post on the chair saying number one. Repeat this procedure with all the other numbers, making sure that every child has a turn. Take off the imaginary uniforms to finish the activity.

Questions to ask
As you take the children for a walk along Red Road, stop by each house and ask them to tell you the number. Before sending individual children out to post the letters, ask who can point to the right house. How many letters are there for number 4 Red Road?

For younger children
Reduce the number of letters per child and use numbers one to five only.

For older children
Add magazines and parcels to the delivery round. Add a selection of simple names (perhaps some of the children's own names) to the addresses and ask the children to read these out before posting them.

Follow-up activities
● Complete photocopiable page 60, drawing lines to match the mail with the houses.
● Make a model of Red Road using construction toys or painted cardboard boxes. Let the children number the houses and put them in the correct places.
● Take the children on a walk down a real street to look for house numbers.

THE BIRTHDAY BOOK

Learning objective
Drama – to learn sorting skills.

Group size
Nine children.

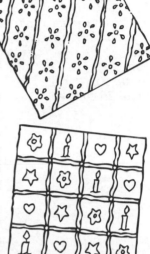

What you need
Three sheets of A4 paper in a ring binder, birthday wrapping paper, scissors, adhesive tape, a gift for the group such as something to eat or play with, a hand puppet, items for three different sorting tasks such as coloured cubes, small toys and scrap materials.

Setting up
Cover the ring binder with birthday paper. On each sheet of A4 paper, write simple instructions for a sorting task, for example *Sort out the coloured cubes into reds, greens and yellows*. Put out the sorting items in three separate boxes in different parts of the room. Hide the gift somewhere in the room. Put the children into three groups.

What to do
Tell the children that it is the puppet's birthday today. Make it look sad. Tell the children that the puppet has been sent a special birthday book. Explain that if the puppet follows the instructions in the book, it will be able to find a special present, but the puppet can't follow the instructions. Ask the children if they will help. Read out the tasks in the book and let the children carry out one task per group. On completion, find the hidden gift and let the puppet share it with the children. Sing 'Happy Birthday' to the puppet and make it look happy.

Questions to ask
Why do you think the puppet looks so sad? Which box will this group need to use, to follow the instructions on this page? What books have *you* been given on your birthday? When the children are sorting, ask Why did you decide to put that in this pile?

For younger children
Keep the group small and work together on one or two simple tasks, such as sorting things by colours.

For older children
Increase the number of tasks per group and make the tasks more challenging.

Follow-up activities
● Use dough to make three kinds of party food such as sandwiches, cakes and sausage rolls, and sort them out onto three plates.
● Make a birthday book for the children, with a sorting task for each child to complete with a friend on their birthday, in order to find a treat.
● Make a birthday book with blank pages and let the children play with it.

OPPOSITES

Learning objective
Dance – to use movements to focus on high and low, near and far.

Group size
Up to 20 children.

What you need
A tambour or similar instrument, a Jack-in-the-box type toy.

Setting up
Make sure the room is suitable for movement activities.

What to do
Stand the children in a circle and tell them to move their hands high in the air and then low near the ground. Now let them crouch down low, and slowly stretch up high. Repeat this again. Show the children the toy. Then tell them to crouch down low and quickly shoot up high. Let them make themselves as small as a mouse and then as tall as a house. Let them make these contrasting movements to the words *Jack-in-the-box, small as a mouse. Jack-in-the-box, high as a house.* Repeat the rhyme and movements once more.

Now tell the children to skip around the room without touching each other and tell them to stop when you bang the tambour. When they have mastered this, tell them to move near to you without touching anyone. Then tell them to skip far away and stop on the tambour signal. Repeat this near and far sequence with other travelling movements, varying your position in the room each time. Finish with a repeat of the Jack-in-the-box rhyme and movement.

Questions to ask
Is a mouse small or tall? Is a house high or low? What will the Jack-in-the-box do when I open the box? How shall we travel next time? Shall we skip, hop, jump, tiptoe or run? How shall we move our hands/arms as we move around the room?

For younger children
Spend several sessions practising stopping on the tambour signal, before tackling the near and far activities. Restrict the travelling to walking or running on tiptoe.

For older children
Ask the children to move other body parts high and low as they travel, for example bottoms and elbows.

Follow-up activities
● Try throwing beanbags or rolling balls towards a marker. See who can get the nearest.
● Using outdoor equipment, such as a climbing frame, ask the children to climb up high or stand down low.
● Focus on the words 'near' and 'far' when using a remote-controlled toy.

NUMBER RHYMES

Learning objective
Drama – to develop a well-known number rhyme.

Group size
Up to 40 children.

What you need
A few hats, scarves or other costumes to represent the characters in a number rhyme such as 'Five currant buns'.

Setting up
Teach the children the chosen rhyme. Assemble the necessary costumes and arrange the children in front of an acting area.

What to do
Act out the original number rhyme putting as many children as possible in costume. For example in 'Five currant buns', the baker can be dressed in an apron and the customers can wear scarves. The currant buns can wear red hats to represent t h e cherries on the top and carry a sign saying one penny. Act out the rhyme twice with the same children and then repeat with another group of children.

Now omit the song and focus on the event in the rhyme. Ask the shopkeeper and the customers to add some simple dialogue such as *Hello, what would you like? One currant bun please. Thank you.* Follow this with a similar sequence, using objects that you might buy in other shops. For example, let five children buy five teddies or toy cars in a toy shop or order five glasses of orange squash in a café.

Questions to ask
Prepare children for the dialogue by asking them questions about appropriate vocabulary. What will the baker say when the children come into the shop? How should the boy or girl ask for a currant bun? Find four or six objects for the other shops and then ask Have I got five things here? Do I need more or have I got too many?

For younger children
Use smaller groups and make up slightly different versions of the original rhyme instead of using dialogue. For example 'Five currant buns in a baker's shop' can become 'Five gingerbread men'.

For older children
Encourage children to develop and extend the dialogue in the shops. Use up to ten things in each shop and use different numbers each time.

Follow-up activities
● Let the children make pictures of the different numerical stages of the rhyme.
● Make up simple hand movements to number rhymes or use those in *Hand Rhymes* by Marc Brown (Picture Lions).
● Make up amusing and unlikely versions of the number rhyme, such as 'Five wriggley worms in a baker's shop'.

MAGIC LANDS

Learning objective
Dance – to explore the numbers two to five.

Group size
Up to 12 children.

What you need
Two to five beanbags for each child, a large box, a mat big enough for all the children to sit on.

Setting up
Place all the beanbags in the box.

What to do
Ask the children to pretend that the mat is a magic carpet that will take them to the land of ... (select a number from two to five). Let each child take the corresponding number of beanbags from the box. Sit the children on the 'magic carpet' and say the words *'Magic carpet, take us to the land of (number 2, 3, 4 or 5) ... Whooosh!'* Announce your arrival and tell the children to place their beanbags around the edges of the room. Make a number dance, by asking the children to move parts of their bodies in different ways, for the appropriate number of times. For example in the land of 'Four' they can jump, wave arms, nod heads and stamp feet four times. Ask the children for more ideas and make these movements into a sequence. Repeat the actions to make a dance. Invite the children to collect their beanbags, before returning home on the carpet with the words *'Magic carpet take us home again ... Whooosh!'* Visit other 'number-lands' on subsequent occasions.

Questions to ask
What parts of our bodies can we move (2, 3, 4, 5) times? How can we move our feet (2, 3, 4, 5) times? How can we move our hands (2, 3, 4, 5) times? How can we move our head... arms... elbows... fingers... (2, 3, 4, 5) times? Shall we move quickly or slowly?

For younger children
Work with small groups and limit the lands to the numbers two and three.

For older children
Visit the lands of numbers from five to ten, taking just one set of five to ten beanbags and use the beanbags in the dance.

Follow-up activities
● Set out the appropriate number of skittles and let the children try to knock them down with their beanbags.
● Invite the children to make and collect things for a display of the chosen number.
● Use the magic carpet to visit the 'land of colours'. Take one hoop for each of the primary colours and place them in different parts of the room. Make up a dance moving towards and away from each coloured hoop.

THREE DIRECTIONS

Learning objective
Dance – to explore three directions: backwards, forwards and sideways.

Group size
Up to 20 children.

What you need
A small drum.

Setting up
Make sure the room is suitable for movement activities.

What to do
Stand the children in a line and take them for a walk around the room, varying the route as you go. Now tell them to go for a walk on their own without bumping into each other. They must stop whenever you bang the drum. Once they have mastered this, tell them to walk towards you until you bang the drum to stop. Point out that they have been walking forwards.

Now ask them to walk slowly backwards into a space, turning just their heads to see where they are going. Repeat this if necessary. Then ask the children to take some steps sideways. Point out how their feet are moving and then let the children try again. Now let them travel forwards, backwards and sideways focusing on different parts of the body such as heels, toes, bottoms or hands and knees. Return to walking and create a game-like situation, where the children walk around the room and respond appropriately as you call out the directions.

Questions to ask
What else can we walk on besides feet? How else can we move along the floor?

For younger children
Work with a small group and concentrate on walking forwards and backwards without bumping.

For older children
Vary the speed of travelling and make each movement involve all three directions one after the other.

Follow-up activities
● Programme a computer toy such as Roamer to move backwards, forwards and sideways.
● Let the children take turns to pretend to be a robot that you, or other children, can direct backwards and forwards for two to five steps at a time, using an imaginary remote control.
● Take turns to move a puppet or toy in different directions.

MRS MUDDLE'S PICNIC

What you need
A bag of picnic utensils, four dolls in a pushchair, clay or dough, an elderly person's hat.

Setting up
Let the children make some picnic food from the clay or dough. Pack up a picnic bag with enough clay food for five people, but pack it so that there are too many plates, and not enough bowls or cups. Put some spare items in a box near the picnic bag.

What to do
Explain to the children that when you are wearing your hat, you will pretend to be an old person called Mrs (Mr) Muddle. Put on the hat and pick up the picnic bag. As Mrs Muddle, tell the children that you are taking the four dolls for a picnic, but when you tried to pack the picnic bag, you got into a muddle. Ask the children to help you sort out the bag.

Empty the bag out and check the number of utensils. Let the children use the spare items to ensure that you have five of everything. Thank the children and ask them if they would like to help you on the picnic. Take the dolls and the children to another part of the room and let the children unpack the bag and share out the food for the picnic. Sing a number rhyme with the dolls, such as 'Five little ducks', before packing away. Take off the hat to stop the drama.

Questions to ask
How many plates/bowls/cups have I put in the bag? Do we need more plates/bowls/cups, or have we got too many? How many more do we need? How many shall we take out? How many sandwiches/cakes did I pack? Will there be enough for all the dolls?

For younger children
Take just two dolls on the picnic and limit the number of items you take with you.

For older children
Pack unequal amounts of food, as well as utensils, and provide a box of spare food to even things out.

Follow-up activities
● Let the children cut out pictures or drawings of five plates, cups and bowls and paste them onto a paper tablecloth.
● Put a picnic bag in a free play area and let the children make their own picnic.
● Make a block graph of favourite picnic food, using five of the children's suggestions.

This chapter provides a range of activities to foster personal and social development. Some are designed to focus on specific issues, such as bullying, loss, bad moods and starting school. Others encourage children to help other people and to work together.

HELPING ON A SNOWY DAY

Learning objective
Drama – to role play helping an elderly person.

Group size
Ten to 20 children.

What you need
A room with enough space for the children to move around, a picture of a snowman, an elderly person's scarf.

Setting up
Put the scarf out of sight.

What to do
Look at the picture of the snowman together and encourage the children to talk about their experiences of playing in the snow and building snowmen. Ask them if they will join you in pretending to build some snowmen.

Pretend that the room is somewhere outside on a snowy day. Suggest that they will need some spades and use the picture to decide what else they will need to make the snowmen. Mime putting these things into imaginary bags. Then pretend to put on warm clothes before walking through deep snow to stand in the middle of the space. Use mime to demonstrate how to build a snowman, before letting the children build their own.

Admire the completed snowmen and then gather the children together. Fetch the scarf and explain that when you put this on, you will pretend to be an elderly person who came out of a nearby house to talk to the children. As the elderly person, you are impressed with the snowmen and enquire how they were made. Then you become sad because your pets have run out of food. You can't get to the shops because of the snow on the path. Ask the children if they will clear away the snow with their spades. When they have finished, thank the children for saving your pets. Take off the scarf to come out of role. Collect the spades and walk home.

Questions to ask
What do you need to make a snowman? What clothes will keep us warm in the snow? As the elderly person, ask How did you build these snowmen?

For younger children
Work together to build a joint snowman, before suggesting that you clear a path for elderly people living nearby.

For older children
Before the drama, talk about ways of keeping warm in the cold weather. Let the elderly person ask the children for advice on this matter in the drama.

Follow-up activities
● Carry out some activities for keeping warm, such as those in *Toddlerobics* by Zita Newcome (Walker Books).
● Read *One Snowy Night* by Nick Butterworth (Collins Picturelions) and *The First Snowfall* by Anne and Harlow Rockwell (Evans Bros).
● Look at the pictures in *The Snowman* by Raymond Briggs (Puffin) and discuss them.

DON'T BE A BULLY

Learning objective
Drama – to raise
awareness of bullying.

Group size
Four to 20 children.

What you need
A puppet able to express happiness and sadness, a story about bullying such as *Topsy and Tim and the Bully* by Jean and Gareth Adamson (Puffin), a quiet space for discussion.

Setting up
Hide the book from view until it is needed.

What to do
Make the puppet look sad. Explain that some children have been unkind to the puppet, but he won't tell you what they have done. Ask the children to guess what's wrong. Make the puppet communicate with the children by whispering the problem to you. Let it respond to the children's guesses by giving details of the bad behaviour, such as continually taking toys or calling names. Introduce the word 'bullying' to describe this behaviour. Ask the children what the puppet can do about this and discuss the implications of each suggestion. Suggest that telling an adult might be a good idea.

Offer to tell the puppet a story about someone else who was bullied. Read the Topsy and Tim story about bullying. Discuss the best solutions and make the puppet appear to be happier. Relate the puppet's problem to the children's own situation and reassure them that they can tell an adult about bullying.

Questions to ask
How do you think it makes children feel if they are bullied? What should you do if someone bullies you? What should you do if you see someone being bullied?

For younger children
Talk about just one specific incident that has made the puppet sad. Talk about kind things that you have seen the children do for each other and suggest others.

For older children
Consider why some children bully others and talk about how some children copy bullies to make friends. When talking about being kind to each other, include caring for family and pets.

Follow-up activities
● Make sad pictures of the puppet being bullied and happy pictures of children being kind to each other.
● Paint sad and happy faces on paper plates and talk about what makes people happy and sad.
● Draw attention to characters in books who show kindness, such as Cinderella's fairy godmother or the dwarves in Snow White.

CELEBRATIONS

Learning objective
Drama – to explore
aspects of different
cultural celebrations.

Group size
Six to 20 children.

What you need
Some books about festivals and celebrations such as 'Autumn and Winter Festivals', and 'Spring and Summer Festivals', *Themes for Early Years* series (Scholastic), a few costumes and props appropriate to the chosen celebration, a space for the children to move around.

Setting up
Choose a celebration appropriate for the time of year. Use books, pictures, artefacts and the children's own experiences to open up a discussion on the sequence of events during the celebration.

What to do
Tell the children that you are going to pretend to prepare for the celebration. Talk about what activities will be appropriate and let the whole group copy you, as you mime these activities. The miming could include cooking special food such as samosas for Diwali or making gifts for the dragon on Chinese New Year. The children could also mime putting up special decorations such as a Christmas tree. Talk about each activity first, before miming it.

After the preparations, ask the children to pretend to take part in the celebration. If possible, act out the events as if it they were happening to the whole group. Only use costumes and props if really necessary. For example, the children may need to walk under the cover of a sheet to represent the Chinese New Year Dragon, as it parades down the street searching for gifts.

Questions to ask
Tell the children how to make any special food and ask How shall we pretend to make this food? When talking about making special things or doing special things ask How shall we pretend to make or do these things? During the celebration ask What happens next? How shall we pretend to do the next part?'

For younger children
Mime just one or two simple preparations and make a tableau of a moment from a celebration instead of acting out the whole process. Use costumes and props if appropriate.

For older children
After miming the preparations, divide the group into two and let them perform the actions to each other.

Follow-up activities
● Let small groups of children take turns to dress up for a tableau of the celebration. Take photographs to encourage recall and reflection.
● Encourage the children to record their activities in pictures and use these to make a book about the celebration.
● Make a version of something connected to the celebration such as clay divas or painted Easter eggs.

COPY CATS

Learning objective
Dance – to encourage co-operation and taking turns.

Group size
Six to 12 children.

What you need
A space for the children to move about, some recorded music with a strong beat such as the track 'One Trick Pony', on the album of the same name, by Paul Simon.

Setting up
Set up the music ready to start. Stand the children in a circle.

What to do
Tell the children to copy you as you carry out a series of stationary movements such as jumping, hopping, stamping, stretching, bending or wriggling. Invite each child in the circle to make a movement for the rest to copy.

Now lead the children in a line around the room. Explain that they must walk behind you until you say 'Stop'. Focus on not touching each other and keeping in a line. Develop this by telling the children to copy your movements, as you lead them in a 'copy cats' dance, accompanied by the music. Include a variety of movements such as skipping, marching, creeping and galloping. Call out each movement as you start. Now invite the children to take turns at being the leader. To avoid any unsafe practice, ask each leader to show everyone how they intend to move, before they start. Less confident children may need some suggestions.

Finally, lead the children back into the circle on tiptoe, without the music. Tell them to sit down and let them copy you as you finish with gentle hand movements.

Questions to ask
Can you copy this movement? What do we call it? Encourage the children to use the correct terms to describe how they are moving and travelling.

For younger children
Limit the travelling to walking behind others, without touching. Let the children take turns to lead the walking, accompanying the leader if necessary.

For older children
Lead the line in different directions such as sideways and backwards. Make movements fast and slow, or high and low. Encourage leaders to be ambitious in their movements.

Follow-up activities
● Find a place where a light casts shadows and let the children experiment with moving their hands or bodies to make different shadows.
● Clap out very simple rhythms for the children to copy.
● Say individual lines from nursery rhymes, and let the children copy your speech.

SAYING GOODBYE

Learning objective
Drama – to learn to
cope with parting from
loved ones.

Group size
Ten to 15 children.

What you need
A room with enough space for the children to move around, a scarf length of grey, brown or black fur fabric, two cheerful singing and dancing games such as 'Ring-o-ring-o-roses' and 'The hokey cokey' in *Oranges and Lemons* by Ian Beck and Karen King (Oxford University Press), a favourite song, a picture book, a chair.

Setting up
Place the chair at one end of the room and place the fur scarf and the book on the chair.

What to do
Ask the children if you can use the scarf to pretend to be an animal called Ben, who has come to play with them. Put on the scarf to play the part of Ben, who is a kindly creature. As Ben, ask the children if they will play the singing and dancing games with you. Show obvious pleasure at the children's enjoyment in the games.

After the games, sing a favourite song and then share the book. Now tell the children that you have to go away for a long time and you may not come back. Tell them that you will always remember this happy day. Leave them the book to remember you by. Slowly turn your back and take off the scarf, saying 'Ben left the children and they never saw him again'. Talk about how everyone feels and suggest that the book will remind them of the happy day with Ben.

Questions to ask
How do you feel now that Ben has gone? What did you like best about your day with Ben? What do you think Ben will remember most about his day with us?

For younger children
Work with a small group. After Ben has left, focus on remembering happy times in general and encourage the children to recall their own happy times.

For older children
Talk about how Ben has shown friendship, by sharing and giving. Read *Badger's Parting Gifts* by Susan Varley (Picture Lions) instead of the picture book.

Follow-up activities
● Show the children some old photographs and talk about memories.
● Read *Grandma's Bill* by Martin Waddell (Simon and Schuster).
● If appropriate, let the children share happy memories of pets that have now died.

THE BAD MOOD

Learning objective
Drama – to develop an awareness of bad moods and their consequences.

Group size
Ten to 20 children.

What you need
A teddy, a hand puppet called Sam, two birthday presents for the teddy, a pen, wrapping paper and sticky tape.

Setting up
Wrap the presents. Write on one present, 'To Teddy, love from Sam' and on the other write, 'To Teddy, love from the children'. Put the teddy and the present from the children in a central position in the room. Place Sam and Sam's present, out of sight.

What to do
Ask the children to join you in pretending to hold a birthday party for Teddy in Teddy's house. Ask them to help prepare the food and encourage them to make suggestions. Use mime to demonstrate each task, before letting the children begin. Inspect and praise the completed work. Explain that everyone is invited to the party except Sam the puppet, because Sam spoiled Teddy's party last year by being in a bad mood. Discuss what Sam did to spoil the party such as snatching food, cheating at games or being unkind.

Now bring out Sam, who communicates by whispering to you. Sam has a present for Teddy and wants to know what time the party starts. Let the children tell Sam why she has not been invited. Sam apologises and gives Teddy the present. Let Sam watch how the children behave at the party. Open the presents for Teddy, pretend to eat the food, play a party game and finish by singing Happy Birthday.

Questions to ask
What food shall we make for the party? Can you guess what Sam did to spoil the party? How do you think this made everyone feel? Why do you think Sam was in a bad mood?

For younger children
Hold the party in the home corner with a smaller group.

For older children
Let each child make a birthday card to give to Teddy during the drama.

Follow-up activities
● Read *Bad Mood Bear* by John Richardson (Arrow Books) and *What Feels Best?* by Anita Harper and Susan Hellard (Picture Puffin).
● Discuss how to identify and cope with bad moods in the group.
● Let Sam offer an explanation for her bad mood, such as feeling tired or upset.

MIMING TOGETHER

Learning objective
Drama – to work
together to mime
actions in a sequence.

Group size
Six to 20 children.

What you need
The words and accompanying actions to 'Here we go round the mulberry bush' from *Oranges and Lemons* by Ian Beck and Karen King (Oxford University Press). Pictures of gardening tools and gardens. A rhyme or song about a garden, such as 'Mary, Mary, quite contrary'.

Setting up
Stand the children in a circle. Put the pictures to one side.

What to do
Sing and mime the actions to 'Here we go round the mulberry bush'. Now mime the actions in more detail, without the song and let the children copy you as you narrate. A morning wash for example might include rolling up your sleeves, reaching for the soap, turning on the taps, washing your hands and face and reaching for the towel to dry yourself.

Now show the children the gardening pictures and talk about what activities are involved in gardening. Mime these activities with the children, talking them through the details as you go. Activities could include putting on boots, opening the shed for tools, mowing the lawn, digging, planting, watering and weeding. Complete the work by tidying away, taking off boots, washing hands and admiring the garden. Finish by moving round the circle holding hands, singing a song about a garden such as 'Mary, Mary, quite contrary'.

Questions to ask
What do you use to wash your face... clean your teeth... eat your breakfast? What clothes shall we put on to work in the garden? What tools do we need to dig the garden... plant some seeds... mow the grass... water the flowers?

For younger children
Restrict the activity to the song and activities for 'Here we go round the mulberry bush' but adapt it to include more detail such as 'This is the way we turn on the taps ...squeeze out the toothpaste ...put on our clothes' and so on.

For older children
Using the children's suggestions, negotiate what should be included in the garden. Encourage more ambitious ideas such as building a fence or a pond.

Follow-up activities
● Let the children invent their own actions to familiar nursery rhymes.
● Let some children work together to create a picture of a garden, using the photocopiable page 'Miming Together' on page 61.
● Talk about the importance of regular washing and cleaning teeth.

STARTING SCHOOL

Learning objective
Drama – to use a
puppet to open up
discussion on starting a
new school or class.

Group size
Ten to 20 children.

What you need
A glove puppet that can show happiness and sadness.

Setting up
Sit the children in the story corner. Put the puppet out of sight.

What to do
Talk to the children about starting a new school or class. Bring out the puppet and explain that he is feeling sad about going to his new school. Ask the children if they can guess why the puppet feels sad about this. Let the puppet nod in agreement if the children make appropriate suggestions. Add suggestions of your own if the children find this difficult.

Use the puppet's situation to discuss any fears that the children might have about starting school. Help the children to give the puppet advice on how to handle any perceived problems such as getting lost or being pushed in the playground. Tell the puppet about making new friends and let two children act out how to ask someone to play with you. Act out other things for the puppet, such as answering the register or changing for PE.

Questions to ask
What do you think will be the best thing about starting school? What will be different at your new school? Why is the puppet feeling so sad about starting school? What can he be worried about?

For younger children
Concentrate on learning to become independent in the present environment and make the puppet sad because he does not know how to do things for himself. Let the children demonstrate how to do some of these things.

For older children
Make the puppet unhappy now he is at school. Use this to open up a discussion on things that can make children unhappy during their first year at school.

Follow-up activities
● Take the children on a visit to the new school to point out the similarities and differences to their existing environment.
● Let the children make a picture book for the puppet about starting school.
● Let each child make their own 'Ready for school' book with pictures of things they can do such as putting on their own coat, fastening shoes and reading their own names.

Many of the imaginary situations used in dance and drama require children to concentrate on aspects of the world. In the activities in this chapter, children need to think carefully about the movement of insects or animals and solve problems connected with healthy living and the environment.

JUNGLE JOURNEY

Learning objective
Drama – to focus on the distinction between pets and wild animals.

Group size
Up to 30 children, depending on space.

What you need
A large space, a picture of a jungle with monkeys, elephants, parrots and other jungle creatures, a copy of 'Row, row, row your boat' in *This Little Puffin* (Young Puffin), a thin scarf.

Setting up
Put the scarf to one side for later.

What to do
Talk about the jungle picture and ask the children to join you in pretending to go on a journey to a jungle, to take photographs of the creatures. Tell the children that some people try to take jungle creatures away for pets. Explain why these creatures do not make good pets and why they can become unhappy. Ask everyone to pretend to get into a rowing boat to travel to the jungle. Mime this without moving from the spot. Sing 'Row, row, row your boat' as you row. Step out of the boats and tie them up. Now lead the children around the room, as if walking through the jungle. Suggest that everyone takes photographs of the creatures . Stress the need to be quiet, so as not to frighten the creatures away. Walk back to the boats, untie them and sit inside.

Tell the children that before they left the jungle, someone came to speak to them. Tell the children that you will pretend to be this person when you wear the scarf. Use the scarf to play the part of someone looking for pets. Ask the children for advice on which jungle creatures would make good pets. Leave when the children have explained why the jungle creatures are unsuitable. Take off the scarf to come out of role. Climb into your boat and sing the rowing song as you row back.

Questions to ask
As the children take photographs, ask them what they can see. What colour parrots can you see? What are the monkeys doing in that tree? In role as the visitor ask questions such as What's wrong with taking an elephant home?

For younger children
Simplify the drama by omitting the person looking for pets.

For older children
Make the walk through the jungle more adventurous by crossing imaginary rope bridges, wading through water and cutting back low branches as you walk.

Follow-up activities
● Read and discuss *Dear Zoo* by Rod Campbell (Picture Puffin).
● Recreate the special sounds that jungle creatures make. Use *Walking Through The Jungle* by Julie Lacome (Walker Books).
● Let the children make sets of creatures that make bad pets and creatures that make good pets, using pictures or models.

CARING FOR PETS

Learning objective
*Drama – to focus on
the needs of the more
popular pets.*

Group size
*Up to 30 children,
depending on space.*

What you need
A room with space to walk around, some pictures
of a variety of pets including a dog.

Setting up
Place the pictures where the children can see them.

What to do
Look at the pictures of pets and talk about caring for them.
Ask the children to pretend that everyone in the group has a pet
dog. Everyone must decide what their dog looks like and give it a
name. Let the children copy you as you talk them through the
following mime sequence:
Stroke the dog/put a collar and lead on it/set off walking with your
dog/come to a busy road/tell the dog to sit while you wait to cross/
walk the dog safely over the road/come to a field/let the dog off the
lead/throw a ball for the dog to bring back to you/say 'drop it' to
make the dog give the ball back/throw the ball again and see what
happens/call your dog and put it on the lead/retrace the walk back/
feed the dog and give it some water.
   Now decide on a pet in a cage and talk about how to clean and
feed it. Let each child copy you as you mime cleaning out the cage
and feeding the pet.

Questions to ask
What does this pet need to keep fit and well? How big is your dog?
Show me by putting your hand on its head to pat it. What is the best
thing to give our dogs for dinner? How do we clean out a cage?

For younger children
Make the sequence shorter focusing on just the dog.

For older children
Talk about training dogs with praise and reward. Let them mime
training their dogs to sit at the roadside. Talk about why you
must sometimes keep dogs on a lead.

Follow-up activities
● Let the children
help you to write a
booklet of advice for
pet owners. Let the
children draw some
of the illustrations.
● Talk about caring
for small pets using
pictures from
information books,
such as *Small Pets –
by Rose Hill (Usborne).
● Cut out pictures of
pets and paste them
next to pictures of
some of the food the
pets eat.

CATERPILLARS AND BUTTERFLIES

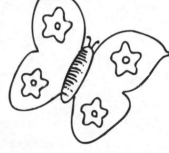

Learning objective
Dance – to use movements associated with the life cycle of the butterfly.

Group size
Up to 20 children.

What you need
A room suitable for movement activities, a toy caterpillar made from a stuffed green stocking, pictures of caterpillars and butterflies, taped music for creeping movements (such as 'The Sound of Silence' by Simon and Garfunkel), a cassette/CD player, a tambourine.

Setting up
Set up the cassette/CD player ready to play the creeping music. Put the toy out of sight until needed.

What to do
Use the pictures and books to open up a discussion on the life cycle of a butterfly. Tell the children to find a space and curl up tightly, as if they were a caterpillar, inside a little egg. Now tell them to slowly creep out of the egg and stretch along the floor as if they were the caterpillar. Call the children together and bring out the toy caterpillar. Make it move along the floor by curling and stretching. Ask the children to describe what the caterpillar is doing. Tell the children to find a space. Ask them to move by curling up very tight and stretching out very long, like the caterpillar. Repeat this movement to the taped music. Now tell the children to build a cocoon around themselves and rest. Then tell them to nibble a hole in their cocoon and crawl out. Talk about moving like butterflies, gently stretching arms when flying and folding arms when landing. Let the children move like butterflies to the sound of the tambourine. Now repeat all the movements as a sequence.

Questions to ask
What is the toy caterpillar doing? How shall we pretend to build a cocoon round ourselves? How shall we move like a butterfly?

For younger children
Spread the activity over two sessions, to focus on one stage at a time.

For older children
Split the group in half and let them perform the sequence to each other.

Follow-up activities
● Read and discuss *The Very Hungry Caterpillar* by Eric Carle (Picture Puffin).
● Learn rhymes about caterpillars such as 'The Caterpillar' in *Hand Rhymes* by Marc Brown (Picture Lions).
● Make Plasticine models to represent each stage of the butterfly life cycle. Refer to 'Clay and Dough' by Lynne Burgess from the *Learning Through Play* series (Scholastic).

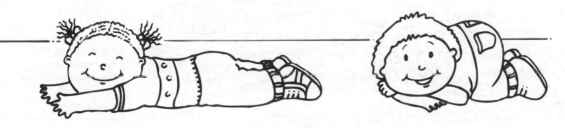

MINIBEASTS

Learning objective
Dance – to draw
attention to the
different movements of
four minibeasts.

Group size
Up to 20 children.

What you need
An opportunity for the children to observe some minibeasts, either on video or in real life. A room suitable for movement activities. Pictures of a centipede, a slug, a woodlouse and an earthworm.

Setting up
Let the children observe the minibeasts, prior to the session.

What to do
Show the children the picture of the centipede and talk about how it moves very fast, taking little steps with its many feet. Tell the children to find a space and ask them to move on all fours, using small quick movements like the centipede. Now show them the picture of the slug. Talk about how the slug moves very slowly, as it eats plants. Tell the children to creep along on their tummies as slowly as they can, eating plants as they move like the slug. Now show them the picture of the woodlouse. Talk about how the woodlouse loves to chomp dead wood as it creeps along on its tiny legs. Ask the children to creep like the woodlouse, using hands and knees. Now show the children the picture of the earthworm. Talk about how this moves along without any legs. Explain that the earthworm cannot see very well, but can feel things and likes to eat dead leaves. Tell the children to wriggle slowly on their tummies like the worm. Repeat all the movements again.

Questions to ask
What is this minibeast doing? Has it any arms like us? Has it any legs? Does it have any wings to fly? Can you show me how you can move like this minibeast?

For younger children
Work with a smaller group and restrict the activity to the contrasting movements of the centipede and the slug.

For older children
Add other creatures with extra movements such as a mole digging or a spider spinning a web. Split the group into four and allocate a different minibeast to each group. Let the creatures move together.

Follow-up activities
● Encourage observation and discussion by making clay models of the minibeasts.
● Play a version of musical statues, moving and stopping as different minibeasts.
● Use percussion instruments to represent the movements of the minibeasts.

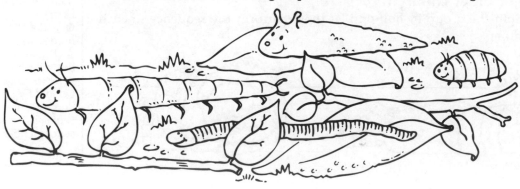

SEASIDE TRIP

Learning objective
Drama – to find out some of the problems caused by litter at the seaside.

Group size
Up to 20 children.

What you need
A picture of children at the seaside. A sign saying 'Open' on one side and 'Closed' on the reverse. A sign saying 'Café'. An apron. A room with space to move around.

Setting up
Place the 'Café' sign and the 'Closed' sign on a wall. Put the apron near the signs. Place the picture within easy reach.

What to do
Ask the children if they will join you in pretending to go to the seaside. Explain that the room will be the seaside in the story. Point out where the sea will be and ask them to pretend that where the signs are is a café. Use the picture to help you decide what to take and then pack your imaginary bags. Mime some seaside activities such as digging sandcastles.

Sit the children down outside the café sign. Explain that you will pretend to be the café owner, when you put on the apron. As the café owner, explain that you have had to close the café garden because litter has blown in from the beach. Explain why the litter is dangerous and unhealthy. Ask the children if they will help. Show them how to pick up litter carefully and put it in the imaginary bins. When the children have finished, thank them and turn the sign to 'Open'. Give each child an imaginary ice cream. Pack up and leave. Take off the apron to come out of role.

Questions to ask
What kinds of litter can you see in the café garden? Why might this be dangerous? Where should people put litter?

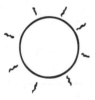

For younger children
Start with the picture and go straight to the activities on the beach. Discover some dangerous litter while on the beach and ask the children to help you pick it up.

For older children
Start and finish with an imaginary journey on a train or bus. Sing a seaside song each time.

Follow-up activities
● Make a collage of the seaside with hidden pieces of litter for the children to find.
● Read *Dinosaurs and All That Rubbish* by Michael Foreman (Puffin).
● Decorate old boxes or tins to use as litter bins. Write the word 'Litter' on them and use them in your room.

MOTHER HUBBARD'S CUPBOARD

Learning objective
Drama – to find out about healthy food, using the rhyme 'Old Mother Hubbard'.

Group size
Six to 10 children.

What you need
Pictures of healthy food, a small table, a copy of the rhyme 'Old Mother Hubbard', an elderly person's scarf.

Setting up
Place the pictures where everyone can see them. Put the table at one side of the room. Put the scarf near the table, but out of sight.

What to do
Recite the rhyme 'Old Mother Hubbard' together. Suggest that the children help Mother Hubbard by filling her cupboard with good things to eat. Talk about the food in the pictures and decide what to put in the cupboard. As food is selected, pretend to put it in imaginary baskets. Ask the children to pretend that the table is Mother Hubbard's cupboard. Put the food into the cupboard.

Now tell the children that you will pretend to be Mother Hubbard (or Mother Hubbard's husband) when you wear the scarf. Ask the children if they will show you how to cook a meal using the food they have brought. Indicate an area of the room as your kitchen. Use mime to demonstrate where the kitchen equipment is. Warn everyone not to rush around in the kitchen. When they have made the meal, sit on the floor and eat it with enjoyment.

Thank the children and take off the scarf to come out of role.

Move the children back to the pictures and talk about what each of the children cooked in the drama.

Questions to ask
Which foods are good for us? Which foods shall we pretend to take to Mother Hubbard's house? How do you cook this? What do you need from the kitchen? (A pan, a knife and so on.)

For younger children
Role play taking enough food for one meal and ask the children to help you cook Mother Hubbard's dinner while she is out. Leave the dinner in the oven for her return. Send the children a thank you note from Mother Hubbard.

For older children
Use an extra table to represent Mother Hubbard's fridge. Decide which items should go in the fridge.

Follow-up activities
● Sort fruit and vegetables by colours.
● Read *Oliver's Vegetables* by Vivian French (Hodder).
● Turn the role play area into the fruit and vegetable section of a supermarket and teach the children the correct names for the produce.

LOOBY LOO

Learning objective
Dance – to name parts
of the body.

Group size
Up to 20 children.

What you need
A copy of the song 'Looby Loo' in *Oranges and Lemons* by Ian Beck and Karen King (Oxford University Press). A large space.

Setting up
Make sure that the room is safe for a movement activity and the children are suitably dressed.

What to do
Tell the children to use their hands to touch their heads, fingers, arms, legs, knees and feet. Tell them to nod their heads very slowly, then shake their heads slowly from side to side. Now tell them to go for a walk around the room and when you say 'Stop' they must wave their hands at you and wriggle their fingers. Tell them to put one arm in the air, then both arms and stretch up tall. Now tell them to sit down slowly and wave their feet at you. Tell them to stand on one leg and ask them to wriggle the lifted foot. Then try with the other leg. Now ask them to wiggle their knees together and apart. Tell them to jump and wiggle their whole bodies. Repeat the above sequence once more. Finally, stand in a circle and sing the Looby Loo song, with the accompanying actions.

Questions to ask
Ask questions which focus on keeping some parts of the body still, while others move. Can you keep your arms still when you wriggle your fingers? Can you keep your legs still when you wiggle your knees?

For younger children
Restrict the activity to a series of action games like the Looby Loo song, such as 'What Can I Do With Both My Hands' in 'Action Rhymes and Games' *Bright Ideas* series by Max de Boo (Scholastic).

For older children
Tell the children to go for a walk around the room and on a given signal, wave a named part of their body in the air and/or put a named part of their body on the floor.

Follow-up activities
● Use games like 'Simon says' to focus on moving different parts of the body.
● Use the photocopiable sheet, 'Looby Loo', on page 62 to encourage the naming of basic body parts.
● Show the children pictures of the bones in the body. Set up a role play area as a medical centre and focus on broken limbs.

MRS MUDDLE'S SUITCASE

Learning objective
Drama – to sort
clothing for hot and
cold climates.

Group size
Up to 20 children.

What you need
An adult's woolly hat. A small suitcase containing clothing for hot and cold climates (sun hat, woolly hat, sandals, gloves). A picture of a holiday destination in a hot climate and a picture of a winter ski resort.

Setting up
Place the pictures where everyone can see them. Place the hat and suitcase out of sight until needed.

What to do
Talk about the pictures of the two different types of holiday. Ask the children to pretend that they are packing a case to go on holiday to a hot, sunny place. Talk about what clothes they might need and let the children pack these into their imaginary cases. Bring out the real hat and suitcase. Tell the children that these belong to Mrs (Mr) Muddle. Explain that she is soon to go on holiday to a hot sunny place. She has tried to pack her case, but keeps getting muddled about what to take. Ask the children if they will help.

Tell the children that you will pretend to be Mrs Muddle when you put on the hat. As Mrs Muddle, remove the clothes from your case and repack it according to the children's advice. Take off the hat to come out of role. Ask the children what Mrs Muddle put in her case and then open it up to check and revise the contents if necessary.

Questions to ask
What clothes would you need for a holiday in a hot, sunny place? What clothes would you need to pack for a cold place? How would you feel if you wore gloves in a hot country? What would happen if you wore sandals in the snow?

For younger children
Work with a small group. Let them help Mrs Muddle sort out her clothes into those for hot days and those for cold days.

For older children
Talk about different ways of keeping cool in hot weather and warm in cold weather.

Follow-up activities
● Cut out pictures of summer and winter clothes from catalogues and paste them onto separate sheets of paper.
● Make the role play area into a travel agent's.
● Collect a variety of dolls' clothes. Ask children to dress one doll for hot weather and another doll for cold weather.

PHYSICAL DEVELOPMENT

Developing children's gross and fine motor skills are the focus of the activities in this chapter. Children are encouraged to develop a sense of space, move their bodies in different ways and in different directions, manipulate puppets and make gifts.

FIND A SPACE

Learning objective
Dance – to build confidence in finding a space for dance work.

Group size
Up to 20 children.

What you need
A large space, a tambour.

Setting up
Make sure that the room is suitable for movement activities and the children are appropriately dressed.

What to do
Let the children follow you as you walk around the room. Now tell them to go for a walk on their own, walking in as many different parts of the room as they can. Tell them they must stop on the beat of the tambour after each of the following movement activities.

Tell the children to walk around the room with their arms stretched out, trying not to touch anyone else. Gather the children around you and tell them to walk to a space where they can sit on their own without touching others. Now tell them to walk back to you once more. Repeat the sequence several times but vary the travelling to include running, skipping or hopping into the space each time.

Develop this activity by asking the children to walk out of their space and then back into it again. Now let them travel around the room in different ways, but on the beat of the tambour they must find a new space and sit down.

Questions to ask
Can you touch anyone else in your space? Can you find your space again if you walk away? Can you find a new space in the room?

For younger children
Concentrate on letting the children move far away from you to a space and then back again. Vary the travelling to include skipping, hopping and jumping to a space.

For older children
Ask the children to run to a space, and then turn slowly on the spot, followed by running to another space and jumping high on the beat of the tambour. Think of ways of moving inside a space.

Follow-up activities
● Let children explore the space around their bodies by clapping their hands together all around themselves.
● Ask children to put toys, dolls and objects into spaces.
● Play games where children stand alone in spaces, such as 'Mary's alone in the ring' in 'Action Rhymes and Games', by Max de Boo from the *Bright Ideas* series (Scholastic).

WOODEN SPOON PUPPETS

Learning objective
Drama – to develop
confidence in
manipulating wooden
spoon puppets.

Group size
One child per story
character.

What you need
A copy of a well-known story or rhyme, one wooden spoon per character in the story, felt-tipped pens or crayons, scissors, adhesive tape, thin card, a clothes line or rope, a curtain or sheet.

Setting up
Hang the clothes line across part of the room, at a height just above the children's heads. Drape the curtain over the line.

What to do
Tell the children that you are going to make some wooden spoon puppets. Draw, colour and cut out bodies for spoon characters from card. Draw appropriate facial features onto the backs of the spoon heads. Place the card body on a flat surface, with its back towards you, and using a piece of adhesive tape, about 4cm long, tape the body to the handle of the spoon. Keep the body flat on the surface while you tape the handle, so that the body will hang straight. Press the tape to the spoon handle and then to both sides of the body. Repeat for all the spoons.

Give each child a spoon puppet. Let two or three children at a time practice walking slowly behind the curtain with their puppets, so that the audience can see the faces of the puppets. Then let the children practise moving their puppets in different ways such as running forwards, walking slowly backwards or jumping up and down. Now tell a simplified version of your chosen story for the children to act out with their puppets. Let the children concentrate on the movements, rather than the words.

Questions to ask
Can you turn your puppet so that everyone can see it's face as you walk along? Can you make your puppet run very fast? ...walk slowly backwards? ...jump up and down?

For younger children
Dispense with the curtain and let the children move their puppets spontaneously, as you tell the story or rhyme.

For older children
Let the children work in pairs to make two puppets walk along together. Then let the children add appropriate speech.

Follow-up activities
● Let two to four children play freely with the puppets.
● Repeat the activity with finger or hand puppets.
● Cut out a TV screen shape from the front of a large cardboard box. Open up the back and let the children move their puppets across the 'screen'.

THERE AND BACK

Learning objective
Dance/drama – to explore movements on a physically strenuous journey.

Group size
Up to 20 children.

What you need
A large space.

Setting up
Make sure that the room is suitable for movement activities and the children are appropriately dressed.

What to do
Organise the children in a line and tell them to follow you as you walk round the room. Warn them to stop when the person in front of them stops. Practise stopping and moving on, as you walk. Now ask the children to pretend that they are going on a long walk through a forest. Tell them to walk behind you as you lead the way. Stop at various times to announce different obstacles and talk about ways of moving through them. These could include pushing away low branches with hands and arms, leaping over a stream on stepping stones; walking up a steep hill with slow steps, climbing a mountain on hands and feet; crossing a narrow wooden bridge with arms outstretched to balance, picking your feet up as you walk along a muddy path.

Finally, stop to announce that it has started to rain and suggest that you make your way back. Retrace your journey back along the muddy path and over the bridge. Walk backwards on hands and feet to climb down the mountain and walk with small steps to keep from falling down the hill. Finish with jumping over the stones and walking under the low branches. Now repeat the sequence, with only brief stops to announce the obstacles.

Questions to ask
How can we use our hands and arms to push the branches away? Who can show us how to leap over these stones? What can we do with our arms to help us balance on the bridge?

For younger children
Work with a small group and restrict the journey to the stepping stones, bridge and steep hill.

For older children
Develop the movements into a dance sequence.

Follow-up activities
● Paint pictures of the various parts of the story and make these into a story book.
● Let pairs of children play the journey game 'There and back' on photocopiable page 63.
● Read *We're Going on a Bear Hunt* by Michael Rosen and Helen Oxenbury (Walker Books) and invent actions to fit the story.

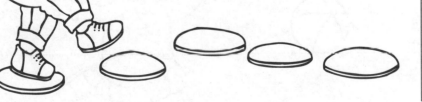

AT THE PARK

Learning objective
Drama – to role play
some physical activities.

Group size
Up to 15 children.

What you need
A large space, pictures of children playing in a park.

Setting up
Make sure that the room is suitable for movement activities and the children are appropriately dressed.

What to do
Use the pictures to talk about playing in a park. Ask the children to join you in pretending to go on a visit to a small park. Pretend to pack imaginary bags with balls, skipping ropes and bread for the ducks. Ask the children to pretend that the room is the park and tell them to sit down on the grass. Demonstrate how to mime playing with a ball by throwing it gently up in the air or bouncing it. Discourage the children from kicking the ball as it may get lost, or hurt someone. Let the children pretend to play with a ball each on the grass. Repeat the activity with the skipping ropes.

Tell the children that there are some swings in the park. Demonstrate how to mime playing on a swing by running backwards and forwards with small steps, to imitate the swinging movement. Tell them to play carefully on the swings. Now stand everyone in a circle, around the duck pond and let them pretend to feed the ducks. Sit the children at the side of the room to end the drama.

Questions to ask
Can you remember what we brought to play with? Why must we never run near the swings? What did you like best about our trip to the park?

For younger children
Replace the swings with a version of 'Here we go round the mulberry bush' using the activities, for example 'This is the way we play with a ball ...skip with a rope ...feed the ducks'.

For older children
Let the children play ball in pairs and skip together in groups. Let them pretend to play on other playground equipment such as a roundabout or a climbing frame.

Follow-up activities
● Read *Topsy and Tim Go to the Park* by Jean and Gareth Adamson (Puffin).
● Paint pictures of the activities and make a book for the book corner called 'Our day at the park'.
● Let small groups of children play freely with real versions of the items they took to the park.

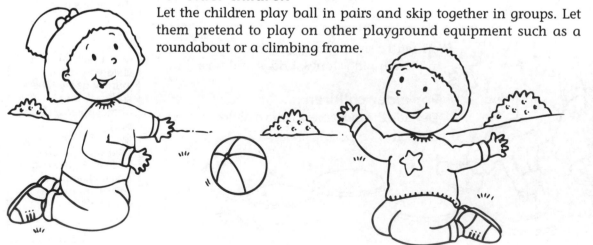

SLEEPING BEAUTY

Learning objective
Drama – to develop fine manipulative skills.

Group size
Up to 20 children.

What you need
A copy of the story of 'Sleeping Beauty', *Favourite Tales* series (Ladybird, a doll wrapped in a white sheet in a cot, a crown or cloak for an adult to play the part of a queen (or king), card, paper, crayons, reclaimed materials.

Setting up
Set out some art materials. Read the story of Sleeping Beauty to the children and ask them to pretend that they have been invited to Sleeping Beauty's christening, which will take place later in the day. Explain that the doll will be the baby princess, in her cot at the christening.

What to do
Let each child use the craft materials to make a christening gift for Sleeping Beauty. Gifts might include decorated jewellery boxes, paper flowers, clay ornaments, paintings or picture books. Encourage the children to use their own ideas and to attempt to make their gift independently. Write the children's names on the completed gifts and keep them in a safe place.

When it's time for the 'christening', hand out the gifts to the children and tell them to sit around the cot. Explain that you will pretend to be Sleeping Beauty's mother (or father) when you wear the cloak or crown. In role as the queen (or king), invite each child to tell everyone what they have brought for the baby and place their gift beside the cot. Make a positive comment about each gift. Take off the cloak or crown to finish the drama.

Questions to ask
What kinds of things could we make for a baby princess like Sleeping Beauty? Tell me about the present you are making for Sleeping Beauty. Why is it a good present for her? What can you use to make your present look even better?

For younger children
Work with a small group and wrap each present. Let the queen try to guess what the present is, before unwrapping it for the princess.

For older children
Use another cloak to pretend to be the wicked fairy. Ask the children to advise you on what you should do and say, before you take on the role.

Follow-up activities
● Talk about what happened next in the story, when the wicked fairy put a spell on the princess.
● Bring in a christening robe and other items and talk about christenings.
● Sing and dance 'There was a princess long ago' in *Oranges and Lemons* by Ian Beck and Karen King (Oxford University Press).

FREEZE AND GO

Learning objective
Drama – to act out
parts of nursery
rhymes.

Group size
Up to 20 children.

What you need
Copies of three or four well-known nursery rhymes with some potential for mime such as 'Jack and Jill', 'Goosey, Goosey Gander', 'Little Miss Muffett' and 'The grand old Duke of York'. A large space, a tambour.

Setting up
Read the rhymes to the children before the activity. Make sure that the room is suitable for movement activities.

What to do
When you bang the tambour and say 'Go', tell the children to walk around the room without bumping into anyone else. When you bang the tambour again and say 'Freeze', they must stop still like statues, until you tell them to sit down. Reinforce the positive behaviour of those children who keep their bodies still on the freeze command. Repeat the activity several times, using the same Go/Freeze words but ask the children to carry out different actions from nursery rhymes each time. For example, carrying a bucket up a hill ('Jack and Jill'), walking up some steep stairs ('Goosey, Goosey Gander'), eating a bowl of food and noticing a spider ('Little Miss Muffett') and marching up and down a hill ('The grand old Duke of York'). Remind the children of the rhyme and make suggestions for the mime and movements each time, before carrying them out. Talk the children through the actions as they move and hold the freeze for a few seconds at the end of each section. Now repeat all the actions, without the intervening discussions.

Questions to ask
How shall we make it look like we are ...climbing up a hill with a bucket ...walking up some steep stairs ...eating our curds and whey, then noticing a spider ... marching up a hill ...marching down a hill? How will our faces look? Show me!

For younger children
Keep to one or two rhymes, and act out the main events in sequence.

For older children
Use more rhymes and give the children longer sequences or whole rhymes to act out before freezing in position.

Follow-up activities
● Let the children help you to invent finger movements to the rhymes.
● Make a book of the rhymes used in the drama and ask children to draw pictures of the events to illustrate it.
● Reinforce the freeze concept by playing musical statues.

TEDDY'S BIRTHDAY SURPRISE

Learning objective
Drama – to develop
fine manipulative skills.

Group size
Six to eight children.

What you need
A large teddy, one doll or teddy for each child, a bag of clothes to fit the dolls and teddies. Fabric adhesive, scissors and a collection of small pieces of fabric and materials suitable for party clothes. White card and drawing materials. A dolls' teaset and a tablecloth. A camera.

Setting up
Set out the fabric and materials. Put the large teddy in the story corner with his face to the wall. Put everything else to one side.

What to do
Gather the group in the story corner. Explain that today is teddy's birthday but he is sad because he thinks that his toy friends have forgotten. Suggest that the children hold a surprise party for teddy and his friends. Ask the children if they will make the dolls' clothes into party clothes for the dolls and teddies.

Give the children one toy each and some clothes and let them decorate the clothes using the scissors, adhesive and other materials provided.

Draw outlines of sandwiches and cakes on the card and let the children colour and cut them out for the party. Decorate some clothes for the main teddy, as a birthday present. Set the table using the teaset and tablecloth and dress the teddy in his new clothes. Let each child hold their toy during the party. Sing 'Happy Birthday' and comment on the toys' beautiful clothes. Finish the party by taking a photograph of the children holding the toys.

Questions to ask
What materials will look good for the party? What else could your doll wear? Will you need to make this piece of material smaller or is it the right size?

For younger children
Let children make hats for the toys instead of decorating the clothes.

For older children
Provide a wider range of materials and encourage the children to plan how they might decorate the clothes before they start.

Follow-up activities
● Read *Worried Arthur* by Joan Stimson (Ladybird).
● Look at catalogues and decide which clothes would be appropriate for a party. Cut these out and display them with the photographs of the toys at teddy's party.
● Talk about fancy dress parties and what people wear to these.

BOUNCE TIME

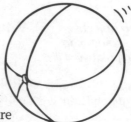

Learning objective
Dance – to explore
bouncing.

Group size
Up to 20 children.

What you need
A ball, a large space, a tambour.

Setting up
Put the ball and tambour to one side of the room. Make sure that
the room is suitable for movement activities and the children are
appropriately dressed.

What to do
Tell the children to find a space so that everyone has enough room to
move. Bounce the ball and tell the children to copy what it does.
Repeat the activity, encouraging the children to bounce on the balls
of their feet, with feet together and springy ankles and knees. Suggest
that they make both high and low bounces. Now ask the children to
watch the ball as you bounce it around the room.

Put the ball away and tell the children to carry on bouncing around
the room like the ball. Encourage them to bounce lightly on two feet
together with springy movements. They must stop when they hear
the tambour. Then ask the children to bounce around the room with
high bounces. Encourage them to give a big push from the floor to
start off each bounce and bend their knees on landing. Finish by
asking them to pretend to bounce a ball on the spot with high and
low bounces.

Questions to ask
Can you copy the ball? Can you bounce with two feet together? Can
you bounce with light springy bounces? Can you bend your knees
when you land?

For younger children
Concentrate on bouncing on the spot to music and make the activity
into a game like musical bumps.

For older children
Let the children watch a balloon as it bounces very lightly. Let half
the group sit around the room as the other half bounces among
them like a balloon full of air.

Follow-up activities
● Read *Bouncing* by
Shirley Hughes
(Walker Books).
● Make a collection
of different sized
things that bounce,
such as small rubber
balls and large beach
balls.
● Make sets of
things that bounce
and things that do not.

CREATIVE DEVELOPMENT

Opportunities for children to create sounds and stories, using musical instruments and costumes are included in this chapter. The activities also encourage children to express themselves in movement, as they attempt to represent actions, toys and creatures in mime and dance.

MOVING CREATURES

Learning objective
Dance – to move imaginatively, exploring the movements of three creatures.

Group size
Up to 20 children.

What you need
Pictures of a cat and an elephant, a snake made from a stuffed stocking, a tambour and a tambourine. A large space.

Setting up
Put the pictures, snake and instruments to one side. Make sure that the room is suitable for movement activities and the children are appropriately dressed.

What to do
Show the children the picture of the cat and talk about how cats move. Ask the children to close their eyes and pretend that they are stroking a cat, feeling its head, back and tail. Now ask them to walk on hands and feet, like a cat walking quietly and softly along a wall. Then tell the children to be the cat, as it stretches and curls up to fall asleep on the wall.

Call the children to you and show them the picture of the elephant. Talk about how elephants move and ask them to stamp their feet heavily, like an elephant. Now tell them to stamp around the room to the beats of the tambour, lifting their knees high as they stamp like elephants. Explain that elephants can also walk slowly and gently, waving their trunks as they move. Tell the children to move slowly around the room like elephants, using one of their arms as a trunk.

Bring out the snake and talk about how it wriggles and twists its body, as you move it along the floor. Let the children try wriggling and twisting like a snake, as you play the tambourine. Now repeat all the movements once more without the intervening discussion.

Questions to ask
Who can show us how a cat/elephant/snake moves? Are elephants bigger than a cat? How can you make yourself look big and strong like an elephant? How do snakes move along as they haven't got legs?

For younger children
Make the activity into a game where you call out: Can you move like a ...cat ...elephant ...snake? Include other creatures such as a bird, butterfly or mouse.

For older children
Let groups perform the different creature movements in a set order, to make a dance sequence.

Follow-up activities
● Repeat the activity with creatures chosen by the children.
● Sort toy creatures into two boxes labelled large and small.
● Make clay models of a cat, an elephant and a snake.

SOUNDS LIKE THE THREE PIGS

Learning objective
Drama – to use mime and percussion to illustrate a story.

Group size
Ten to 15 children.

What you need
A copy of 'The Three Little Pigs' *Favourite Tales* series (Ladybird), a whistle, one percussion instrument per child. Group the instruments into those making light sounds to represent straw (tambourine/rainstick/cabasa/windchimes/triangle), wooden sounds (wood block/wooden agogo/castanets/claves/guiro) and hard metallic sounds to represent building tools and bricks (cymbal/cowbell/tambour/snare drum/bongos).

Setting up
Place the book and whistle near the instruments.

What to do
Sit with the children in a large circle. Demonstrate how each of the instruments should be used to make a sound. Put one instrument in front of each child and ask them not to touch the instruments until you say they can. Explain that when you clap your hands they should play their instruments, when you blow the whistle they should stop and put their instruments down. Try this out a few times, until the children learn when to start and stop.

Now read the story of 'The Three Little Pigs'. When you reach the part where the first pig builds a straw house, indicate to the children with the light-sounding instruments to make sounds for straw. The rest of the group must mime actions for cutting straw, twisting straw into bundles and building the straw house. Use the whistle to stop them. Repeat this activity for building the other houses, using the appropriate instruments. Mimes for building the wooden house could include sawing wood, hammering nails and putting in screws. Mimes for building the brick house could include mixing cement and laying bricks with a trowel. Finish by letting all the children play their instruments, as the wolf falls down the chimney.

Questions to ask
Does this drum make a light straw sound or a heavy brick sound? What instruments shall we use for building the wooden house? How shall we pretend to cut straw ...hammer nails ...lay bricks?

For younger children
Spread the activity over four or five sessions to give the children the chance to learn what to do.

For older children
Repeat the activity three times and let the children move round to play a different instrument each time.

Follow-up activities
● Raise and lower your hands to signal playing louder and quieter.
● Use instruments and vocal sounds to accompany parts of *One Stormy Night* by Ruth Brown (Red Fox).
● Make shakers by filling washing-up liquid containers with dried pulses or pasta.

THE SAD DAY

Learning objective
*Drama – to take part
in a role play and
storymaking activity.*

Group size
Six to ten children.

What you need
An elderly person's scarf, a resealed envelope (previously
sent through the post) containing a letter inviting someone
for a hospital appointment, a chair and an acting area.

Setting up
Place the chair in the centre of the acting area and place the scarf on
the chair. Put the letter out of sight, at the back of the acting area.

What to do
Explain that when you put on the scarf, you will pretend to be
an elderly person in her (his) house. Tell the children to watch
carefully until you finish. Put on the scarf and say 'I think I
heard the letterbox. I hope someone has sent me a letter'. Walk
to the back of the acting area. Keeping your back to the children,
pick up the letter and pretend to pick it up from your door mat.
Look pleased as you sit on the chair to open your letter. Gradually
become concerned, as you read out the letter. Tell the children that
you have to go to the hospital to see a doctor. Take off the scarf and
explain that you have now stopped pretending to be this person.

   Talk about the person's feelings and discuss some possibilities
concerning the person's illness. Use the children's ideas to create a
plausible situation. Talk about hospitals and reassure the children
about what might happen next. Then create a role play situation by
inviting some children to play the receptionist and doctor, as you
play the elderly person visiting the hospital.

Questions to ask
How was the person feeling when she (he) read the letter? Who was
the letter from? Why did the letter make her feel so sad? What happens
in hospitals?

For younger children
Work with a smaller group and use a role play area set out as a hospital.

For older children
Dispense with the hospital situation and ask the children to decide
what was in the letter. Use some of the children's ideas to create a
story situation for the role play.

Follow-up activities
● Make a book, with
illustrations by the
children, to describe
the role play events.
● Read books about
hospitals such as
*Topsy and Tim Go to
Hospital* by Jean and
Gareth Adamson
(Puffin).
● Talk about things
that worry people
and reassure the
children where
possible.

TOY DANCE

Learning objective
Dance – to use
imagination to explore
the movements of
three toys.

Group size
Up to 20 children.

What you need
A floppy doll, a toy aeroplane and a string puppet.
A tambourine, a large space.

Setting up
Place the toys in a box and put the tambourine where it can easily be reached. Make sure that the room is suitable for movement activities and the children are appropriately dressed.

What to do
Bring out the floppy doll and make it sit up straight with legs stretched out in front. Ask the children to sit like the doll. Let the doll go and ask the children if they can flop over like the doll. Now make the doll dance. Talk about how the doll's limbs and body flop about as it dances.

Tell the children to find a space and dance like the doll, as you play the tambourine. Then let the children perform their floppy doll dances to each other, half the group at a time. Use this as an opportunity to reinforce any good practice. Praise floppy legs, arms, hands, fingers and bodies.

Now gather the children to watch you fly the toy aeroplane. Compare the stiff straight wings and body, to the floppy movements of the doll. Ask one or two children to demonstrate how to move like the aeroplane. Then let all the children try, using half the group at a time to avoid collisions.

Bring out the puppet and make it jump with legs apart before falling in a heap. Let the children find a space and try to jump and fall like the puppet. Now repeat the movements without the toys, to make a toy dance.

Questions to ask
What is this toy doing? Can you move like this toy? Who can show us how to move like that?

For younger children
Play 'Musical statues' and 'Simon says' using the toy movements.

For older children
Extend the activity to include objects with interesting movement properties such as a piece of elastic, a length of chiffon or a polythene bag.

Follow-up activities
● Play action games about puppets and toys such as 'Punchinello' in 'Action Rhymes and Games' by Max de Boo from the *Bright Ideas* series (Scholastic).
● Play with different floppy toys and small beanbags.
● Sort toys into floppy toys and stiff toys.

IT'S RAINING

Learning objective
Dance – to respond
imaginatively to some
images of a rainy day.

Group size
Up to 20 children.

What you need
Some pictures of a rainy day, a percussion instrument that can make rain-like sounds, such as a rainstick or a tambour, a large space.

Setting up
Put the picture where everyone can see it and put the instrument to one side. Make sure that the room is suitable for movement activities and the children are appropriately dressed.

What to do
Use the picture as a stimulus to talk about rainy days. Demonstrate the sound of the instrument to make the sound of light rain falling. Ask the children to tap their fingers lightly on the floor to make a similar sound. Then tell them to find a space and make the sound of heavy rain by beating on the floor with their hands, beating hands together in the air and beating feet on the floor.

Now ask the children to pretend that the room is full of puddles. Tell them to jump over the puddles with big leaps. Then tell the children to stamp and splash in the puddles. Finally, tell the children to put up an imaginary umbrella and hold on to it tightly, as they walk in the wind. Now use the movements to make the following dance sequence: tap the floor to make light rain; make beating sounds like heavy rain; leap over puddles; stamp in the puddles and walk with an umbrella in the wind.

Questions to ask
What do people wear to keep them dry in the rain? What happens if you stamp hard in a puddle? Why must you hold on tight to your umbrella on a rainy, windy day?

For younger children
Lead the children through the movements in a follow-my-leader formation.

For older children
Add the following movements: run all over the room with light steps to make the sound of gentle rain falling; make continuous fluttering movements with the fingers, moving them up and down the length of the body to suggest the falling rain.

Follow-up activities
● Learn the song and actions to 'I hear thunder' in 'Action Rhymes and Games' by Max de Boo *Bright Idea* series (Scholastic).
● Ask the children to collect objects that they think would float and then test them out in a shallow bowl of water.
● Paint pictures of rainy days and display these with the rhyme 'Rain, rain, go away, come again another day'.

SNOWMEN

Learning objective
Dance – to demonstrate an imaginative response to playing in the snow.

Group size
Up to 20 children.

What you need
Pictures of children playing in the snow and building a snowman, a large space.

Setting up
Put the picture where everyone can see it. Make sure the room is suitable for movement activities and the children are appropriately dressed.

What to do
Talk about playing in the snow and show the children the picture. Talk about what snow feels like. Tell the children to wiggle their fingers like fluttering snowflakes falling to the ground. Encourage them to start with their arms up high and then flutter their fingers to the ground.

Ask the children to pretend that it is a snowy day. Let them pretend to put on appropriate clothing and step outside into the snow. Tell them to find a space and keep warm by stamping their feet, jumping up and down and swinging their arms. Now tell the children to make big footprints in the deep snow. Encourage them to lift their knees high as they walk. Now tell them to gather some snow to make a big snowman. Encourage them to pat the snow down and put some stones on to make a face. Now tell them to dance in and out of all the snowmen, to keep warm. Make a dance sequence from the following movements: flutter fingers like snowflakes; stamp feet and swing arms to keep warm; walk with knees high to make footprints; gather snow and pat down the snowman; dance round the snowmen.

Questions to ask
What can you play in the snow? What does snow feel like? What clothes do you wear to play in the snow? How can we move to keep warm in the snow? What will happen to the snowmen when the weather gets warmer?

For younger children
Adapt the movements to work in a circle formation. Build one big snowman in the centre of the circle and dance around it.

For older children
Ask the children to dance lightly and silently around the room like snowflakes, swirling and twisting as the snowflakes drift and fall.

Follow-up activities
● Read *One Snowy Night* by Nick Butterworth (Collins Picture Lions).
● Read *The Snowman* by Raymond Briggs (Ladybird Books) and talk about how cold things can melt. Melt some ice and talk about what has happened.
● Make model snowmen by covering cardboard tubes with cotton wool, and using pieces of felt for the details.

ON THE BEACH

Learning objective
Dance – to explore activities on the beach, through dance.

Group size
Up to 20 children.

What you need
A picture of people on the beach, a tambour, a large space.

Setting up
Put the picture where everyone can see it and place the tambour nearby. Make sure the room is suitable for movement activities and children are appropriately dressed.

What to do
Look at the picture and ask the children if they have been to the beach and what they like to do there. Talk about the sights, sounds and smells at the beach, as well as the feelings and emotions associated with a visit to the seaside.

Tell the children to find a space and pretend that they are on a beach. Ask one of the children to choose an activity which people like to do on the beach. Explain that when you beat the tambour they must move as if they were carrying out this activity and when you beat it again they must stop. Look for children with good ideas and let them show the group, before adding your own suggestions to develop the movement. Tell the children to try the activity again, using the new ideas. Repeat with three or four other activities. Use the children's ideas but add your own if necessary. Activities could include swimming by moving arms and legs on the floor or walking using arm movements, paddling, digging in the sand, throwing and catching a ball or a frisbee. Conclude the activities by talking about wave movements. Ask the children to move forwards and backwards like the waves. Repeat all the movements to make a beach dance.

Questions to ask
What can you do at the beach? What is it like to run on the sand? Which toys can you take to play with at the beach?

For younger children
Keep to three or four familiar activities such as digging in the sand, paddling in the pools, playing with a ball and eating an icecream.

For older children
Group the children and allocate a different activity to each group. Let the groups perform to each other and freeze on the beat of the tambour, to make an imaginary holiday photograph. Take a real photograph if possible.

Follow-up activities
● Read *Lucy and Tom at the Seaside* by Shirley Hughes (Puffin).
● Make a display of photographs and postcards of beach activities to stimulate discussion.
● Display things to use at the beach (beach ball, bucket, spade) and let children talk about and complete the 'On the beach' photocopiable sheet on page 64.

DRESSING UP

Learning objective
Drama – to role play
using dressing-up items
as a stimulus for
creative storymaking.

Group size
Two to four children.

What you need
A dressing-up box containing scarves, aprons and jackets. A letter, a notepad and pen, four shopping bags and a telephone. A private space with few distractions.

Setting up
Put the box and objects at the side of the working space.

What to do
Ask the children to join you in pretending to be some people in a story. Ask each child to dress up in one or two items from the dressing up box and also choose an item for yourself. Explain that you are going to use some of these objects in the story. Choose one of the following situations or make up your own:

1. The letter is from a friend who is coming to stay. The house must be made ready. Ask questions about what needs to be done and how to do it.

2. Let each child use the phone to order a take-away meal. Play the part of the take-away owner, who has a wide range of foods to offer. When the children arrive to pick up the food, the owner has forgotten what they ordered.

3. Let the children write a shopping list on the pad. They need things for your birthday party. Go to the shops and ask the children to help you read the list. Some things cannot be found. Ask for alternatives or let one of the children be the shop assistant.

Questions to ask
Where will the visitor sleep? How do you do this job? What would you like to order? Would you like some ...? What will we need to buy for the party?

For younger children
Let the children play freely with the clothes and objects. Look for suitable moments to intervene in order to focus and extend the role play.

For older children
Select one object and ask each character what they might use it for. Choose one of the children's ideas as a situation for the role play.

Follow-up activities
● Write the role play as a story and read this to the whole group.
● Leave the clothes and objects for the children to play with on their own.
● Change the objects and observe the children's play. Encourage them to talk about what happened during their play.

PHOTOCOPIABLES

Name _____

Join up shoes and boots to make pairs.
Colour in each pair.

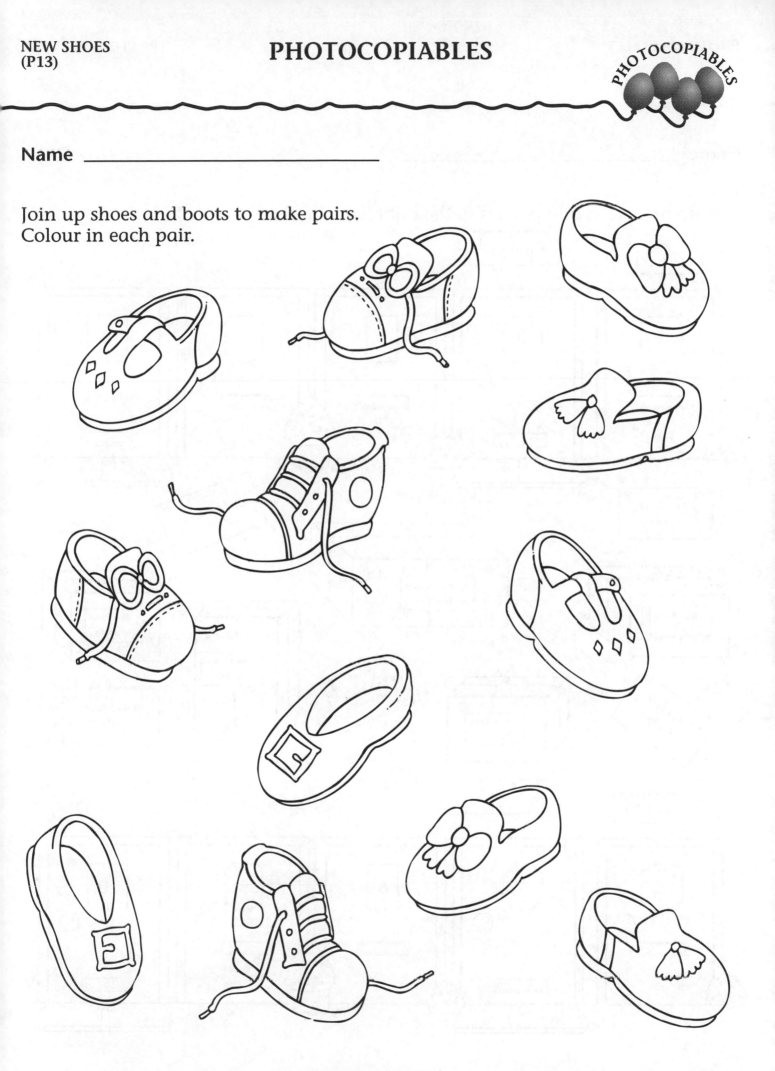

Name _____

Join up the letters and parcels to the right letter boxes.

Name _____

Colour and cut out these garden pieces.

Paste them onto a large sheet of paper.

Let your friends add their garden pieces to make a big garden.

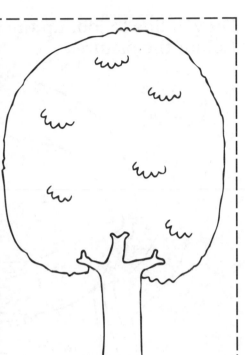

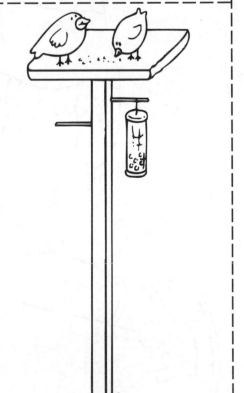

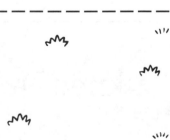

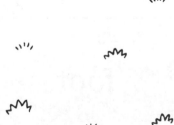

Name _____

Draw a line to join up the words with the right part of the picture.
Colour the picture.

head
hand
arm
leg
knee
foot

Name _____

A game for two children – use counters and cards with numbers 1–3.

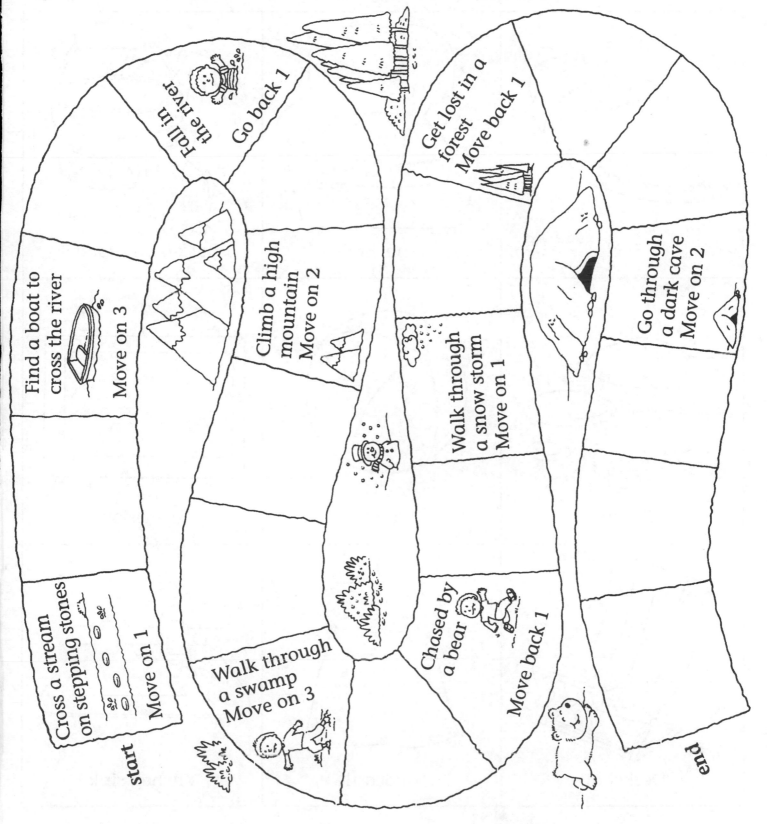

Find a boat to cross the river Move on 3

Fall in the river Go back 1

Get lost in a forest Move back 1

Climb a high mountain Move on 2

Go through a dark cave Move on 2

Walk through a snow storm Move on 1

Cross a stream on stepping stones Move on 1

Walk through a swamp Move on 3

Chased by a bear Move back 1

start

end

Name _____

Colour the things that belong on the beach.

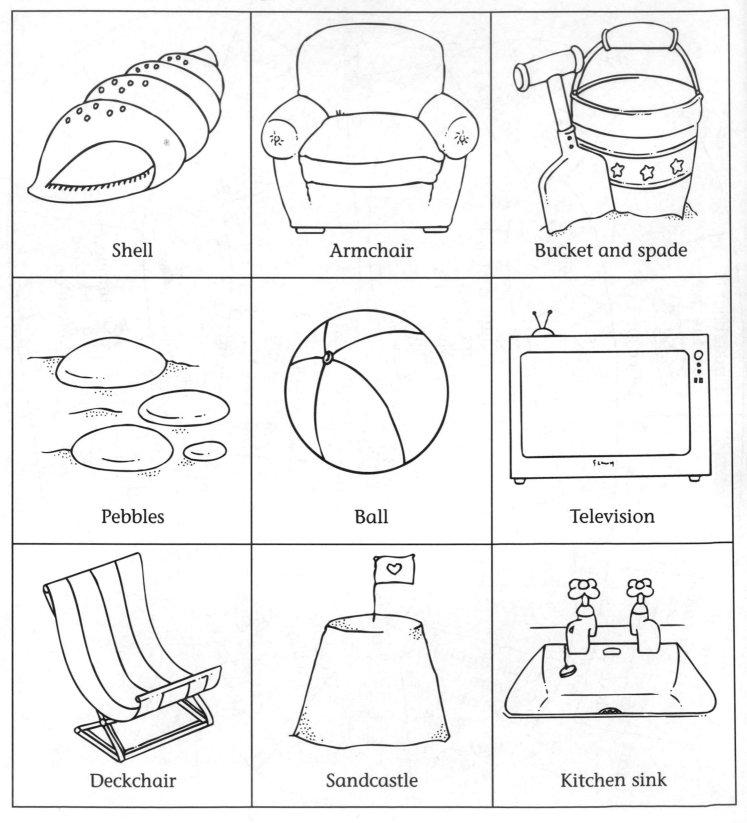

Shell	Armchair	Bucket and spade
Pebbles	Ball	Television
Deckchair	Sandcastle	Kitchen sink